Marked for Life

A Prison Chaplain's Story

Nancy Hastings Sehested

To Eyleen –
who marks my life
with goodness and mercy.
Love,
Nancy

ORBIS BOOKS
www.orbisbooks.com

August 2019

ORBIS BOOKS
Maryknoll, New York 10545

Fathers and Brothers
MARYKNOLL

Founded in 1970, Orbis Books endeavors to publish works that enlighten the mind, nourish the spirit, and challenge the conscience. The publishing arm of the Maryknoll Fathers and Brothers, Orbis seeks to explore the global dimensions of the Christian faith and mission, to invite dialogue with diverse cultures and religious traditions, and to serve the cause of reconciliation and peace. The books published reflect the views of their authors and do not represent the official position of the Maryknoll Society. To learn more about Maryknoll and Orbis Books, please visit our website at www.maryknollsociety.org.

Library of Congress Cataloging-in-Publication Data

Names: Sehested, Nancy Hastings, author.
Title: Marked for life : a prison chaplain's story / Nancy Hastings Sehested.
Description: Maryknoll, NY : Orbis Books, 2019. | Includes bibliographical references.
Identifiers: LCCN 2019004337 (print) | LCCN 2019021768 (ebook) | ISBN 9781608337989 (ebook) | ISBN 9781626983342 (pbk.)
Subjects: LCSH: Sehested, Nancy Hastings. | Prison chaplains—Biography. | Prisoners.
Classification: LCC HV8867 (ebook) | LCC HV8867 .S44 2019 (print) | DDC 259/.5092 [B] —dc23
LC record available at https://lccn.loc.gov/2019004337

For my beloved family near and far

Contents

Acknowledgments

I viewed the complicated world of prison through my small window as a chaplain. These stories are an invitation to see an often hidden world through my encounters in the day to day. I abandoned the writing several times. The tension between bearing witness and keeping confidentiality was too great. Yet I was encouraged by family and friends to offer this vantage point of prison life. I have used fictional names with the exception of my chaplain colleagues. I altered particular characteristics of staff and inmates. I worked with a vast array of administrators, officers, staff, volunteers, and inmates. I have endeavored to be true to the experiences while recognizing the limitations of my singular perspective. This book is not a narrative chronology, but rather a sampling of snapshots from my time at two different prisons over a span of thirteen years.

I have not sought to offer an in-depth analysis of the criminal justice system and the prison industrial complex or to reflect on the inherent racism and classism of those systems. I am indebted to writers like Michelle Alexander and Bryan Stevenson who inform us of the broader picture. I acknowledge their significant influence on my understanding of the social and economic realities of incarceration.

The inmates taught me more than I can ever convey about what it means to be human in the midst of struggles for meaning, identity, and redemption. Each one has a story to tell because each is part of the human family. Any failure in these stories to communicate the astonishing complexities of grief and joy in the lives of these men is mine alone.

I discovered that I could do difficult things when I had allies who could offer perspective and encouragement. I received life-giving doses of wisdom, care, and humor from my chaplain colleagues: Bill Stewart, Bob Fielden, Mark Siler, Mark Menhinick, James Cannon, Danny Hampton, and William Sims.

Prison administrators, officers, and staff labor under the most stressful conditions imaginable on our behalf. I am indebted for what they were able to do to assist my chaplaincy work. Many of their stories of courage, respect, and goodwill have not been adequately rendered in this book.

I am grateful to the volunteers in the religious programs that came through the prison gates week after week. They led religious services, retreats, workshops, and study groups. They brought food and music for special religious holidays. I learned firsthand about the truth and beauty of a diversity of religions through the leadership of volunteers. They regularly walked through the maze of ever-changing policies and procedures to offer a presence and hope to inmates who felt forsaken.

One volunteer in particular partnered with me weekly for seven years to lead a writing class for rotating groups of ten inmates. Full of grace and truth, Mahan Siler was a catalyst for redemptive happenings.

I pastor two communities of faith that have sustained me in prayer and support: Shekinah Gathering in Boone, NC, where I have served as pastoral leader for twenty-two years, and Circle of Mercy congregation in Asheville, NC, where I have served as copastor for seventeen years. They have heard these small stories in the context of the grand story of God's transforming love. My cup overflows with gratitude for their seemingly endless supply of compassion that they spread widely, including to me.

There are friends who have carried hope for me when I could not carry it myself. They challenged me to be true to my own voice while also extending grace to me. Among them are Lynda Weaver-Williams, Annie Beckham, Eyleen Farmer, Nikki Hooser, Kathy Longinaker, Missy Harris, Kim Christman, Stan Dotson, Susan LiVolsi, Bill and Sylvia Everett, Kyle and Jane Childress, Paul and Wendy Hayes, Marty Collier, Carter Garber, Andy Loving, Susan Taylor, Jim Abbott, Jeannie DuBose, Betty Webb, and Jane Medema. Lynda and Jane especially provided countless hours of musing and mulling time.

The three trainings that I conducted in Cuba for prison chaplains through the Cuba Council of Churches gave valuable shape to the content. Muchas gracias, Francisco "Paco" Rodes.

As a preacher I am accustomed to oral communication. I am not as practiced in the written word. The writing has required both editing skills and patience from all who accompanied me on this project. I am grateful to Karen Ackerson of the Writers' Workshop who was the careful editor of my first draft. The experienced writer, editor, and friend, Joyce Hollyday, was indispensable in providing insight in various stages of this book. Margaret Whitt, a retired English professor, came along at just the right time with her welcome enthusiasm as well as her knowledge of book writing.

I am grateful to the staff of Orbis Books for believing in this book. I am particularly grateful for my editor, Jill Brennan O'Brien, for her thoughtful and attentive feedback that made for a better book.

My siblings and their spouses never seemed surprised enough by my vocational choice. Thank you John and Helen, Larry and Marilyn, Abigail, Roger, and Shizue for staying loving and curious. And thank you cousin Pat Rabe for your unwavering belief in this work. My daughters, Jessica and Alayna, plus my grandkids, Jordan, Sydney, Rebecca, and Jonathan, gave a love and joy that never failed to buoy my spirits. Rich, my son-in-law, and his chickens did too.

My sister, Abigail Hastings, was my feisty, funny, and faithful companion through the long labor of writing. Like the best of midwives, her abiding presence, unlimited patience, and enduring spirit of goodness and mercy cheered me to delivery. She loves words. She helped me find words. She loved seeing these words birthed on a page.

My husband Ken was always the first listener of my tales after my long commute home. He has remained the steadfast champion of my calling. He tenderly walked with me through the living of it and the reliving of it as I chronicled the stories. Love and grace abounds.

Surrounded by the presence of so great a cloud of witnesses, I have known the Presence.

Nancy Hastings Sehested
Epiphany 2019

Introduction

It wasn't the blood on the stairs that sent me racing back down the hallway, or the repeated cries of "Oh, my god!" that turned me away. It was simply this: I couldn't breathe. I needed air that was not saturated with pepper spray. With eyes burning, I coughed and sputtered my way back to where I could breathe again. After ten years at the prison, I knew where to go for breathing places.

Two nurses and six officers bolted down the main corridor to the housing unit where the assault had happened. No one invited me to go along, of course. They were the first responders, not me. They had retractable batons, pepper spray, and handcuffs; they could stop the flow of blood or patch a gash of flesh. But me? I was useless. "Nonessential staff."

It was 7:30 on a Sunday morning. I had prepared for the morning worship service, oriented our new assistant chaplain, and checked on the forty volunteers who were leading a weekend spiritual retreat for forty-two inmates. As I walked through the lobby, the sergeant in Master Control announced, "Code 4. Code 4." Inmate-to-inmate assault. Then: "Code Red. Code Red." Medical emergency.

Staff materialized from all directions. I raced with them down the central hallway with the urgency of an ambulance driver. But unlike them, I made a quick U-turn at the red-stained stairwell and parked myself against a wall where I could gulp in air and watch from a distance.

An officer came down the hallway, bent over and gasping for breath. He waved for the control room to pop the outside door. He needed fresh air. It wasn't enough. He stepped outside, threw up in the grass, and returned to duty. "I've never seen so much blood," he said. "I don't know if the guy will make it. Blood was spurting everywhere."

A nurse accompanied by several officers swiftly pushed the victim in a wheelchair toward the gatehouse and the incoming ambulance. When he passed by me, he was still conscious, pressing bloody towels against his neck. I recognized this large muscular man. I couldn't imagine anyone messing with him. Who was the Goliath who attacked him, I wondered?

I didn't know what to do or say. I flung out a prayer. "Luther, God is with you. Mercy to you!"*

I heard a faint "Thanks, Chap," as I watched door after door being opened for him and the emergency crew.

The lieutenant walked toward me and held out a blade about the size of a box cutter with a small plastic handle melted around it. "Chap, this is what sliced him open around his neck and face. It's bad. Real bad."

"Who did it?"

"A guy named Barton. That's all I know."

"Barton? There must be more than one Barton. I can't imagine the Barton I know doing this. He's one of the pipe-bearers for the Native American circle."

"You just never know. Anything can set these guys off."

The prison was immediately put on lockdown. The assistant chaplain, one week on the job, went home with his unpreached sermon tucked under his arm. Our volunteers were allowed to complete the retreat with the inmates. They

---

* All names have been changed and identifying characteristics altered except for the chaplains.

called it a miracle that Luther was alive and prayed that his life be spared.

One day later I saw Luther through his solitary confinement cell window. He showed me his stitches. Almost two hundred trailed down his face and neck. He said he felt lucky to be alive. I agreed that he was truly fortunate and asked him what happened.

"Barton jumped me. That's all I know."

That was not all he knew, I was sure of it—and it was maddening to think I might never know.

I was given permission to see Barton. He was no Goliath, more like an average-sized man in the middle years of his life. He was fully shackled and was led into the conference room by three officers. He slowly eased down into the plastic chair at the far end of the table from me. Chaplain confidentiality permitted me to see an inmate alone, but officers watched closely through the large glass window in the door.

Barton spoke first, sitting up straight in his chair, dignified. He thanked me for coming to see him and apologized for messing up the retreat and the Sunday programs. "I'm truly sorry about that," he said.

"What? You're sorry about the retreat and the Sunday programs? What about Luther?"

He didn't answer.

"I couldn't believe it when I heard you attacked him. What happened?"

Still no answer. I reminded him about his words to his brothers at the pipe ceremonies: "Be careful how you act. What you do reflects back on all of us."

"I know. Please tell the circle how sorry I am."

"The circle? That's it?" I snapped. I pointed out that he had just earned at least five years in solitary confinement. And how could he, I asked, be the same man who only the week before had carved a beautiful treasure box out of soap, a work of art that must have taken hours to create. "Only a few days later, you almost killed a man. It makes my head spin."

"I know, Chap. But I just couldn't let some things go on."

"So this was about defending your honor, your reputation?"

"I was defending more than that. I was defending my life." He spoke calmly. "This is my house for the rest of my life. I've got to live with these guys side by side, in this prison or the next one or the one after that, shipped all over this state, one year after another. This is my life, Chap. I had no other choice."

I was a calamity of emotions. No matter what reason Barton gave me, I wouldn't have found it satisfying. I took a deep breath, placed my folded hands on the table, and leaned over the chasm between us.

"Barton, those are some of the saddest words ever spoken, 'I had no other choice.'" I slammed a hand on the table. "That can't be true. It just can't be." An officer immediately opened the door and asked if I was okay. "Yes, fine," I said confidently. The door closed as the eyes of the officers remained on us.

We stared down at the table through an uneasy silence. The chain around Barton's waist and wrists clanged as he shifted his weight in the chair. "I guess there was a choice. I guess there was."

A few months after I began my chaplaincy work, an inmate called out to me across the yard and quickened his step to catch up to me. "Chap, I thought you left us! Lots of people come for a few months and then they leave. Too depressing. You gonna stay?"

I stayed thirteen years.

It was longer than I could have imagined. I stayed, holding fast to the conviction that truth coupled with mercy can lead to making amends and a new start. The biblical stories of my faith were still alive in me, creating doorways of possibility within the hallways of "no exit" signs. Even in my bleakest of days, I knew that God has a particular fondness for showing up among lives in the ruins, for using us flawed and failed human beings for redemptive purposes. So I became a witness. I bore witness to the tragedy of lives stuck in the misery of a punitive system. I also bore witness to the spirit of hope that emerged from impossible circumstances.

A dear friend and chaplain colleague, Mark Siler, read this manuscript while on the Appalachian Trail. Caught in a drenching rain, Mark and the other hikers took shelter for the night. Bemoaning the thought of putting on wet and cold shoes the following morning, his daughter suggested a trick she'd learned at camp—to stuff the shoes with paper to help them dry out. "Your collection of redemption stories," he wrote, "became the means through which six pairs of hiking shoes made a remarkable transformation from heavy, cold, and wet to light, free, and receptive. May it be so not only for our wet shoes but our easily dampened spirits, particularly in the sea of pain we call prison."

My hope is that these stories shed some light on an unseen world and expand our capacity to engage in the restoration of broken lives.

BEGINNINGS

1

Chaplain Celestial

*It may be that when we no longer know what to do
we have come to our real work,
and that when we no longer know which way to go
we have come to our real journey.*

—Wendell Berry

"Chap Bill, you have a woman here." The gatehouse officer was on the phone to the prison chaplain. I'd arrived for my job interview, but the head chaplain forgot to leave a memo for my clearance.

"Chap, I mean you have a Chaplain something, uh, wait a minute. . ." He peered at me from his glassed-in cubicle. "What's your name?"

"Schested."

"Pardon?"

"Se-hes-ted. "

"Chap Bill, you have a 'Chaplain Celestial' here to see you. Are you expecting her?"

I didn't correct him. Within a few minutes, Chap Bill came to escort me. He was tall with blond hair and a friendly, easy-going manner. "Wanna see the place?" he asked. "I still can't get used to walking into a prison, even after twelve years. I call these concrete buildings 'institutional sin.' Ugly, aren't they? Funny that anyone would think that a concrete world would be good for changing somebody for the better. But you'll find out no one much cares to see these guys get better."

Bill walked and talked fast. For a man who grew up in the mountains, he didn't have the drawl or the slow pace of others. I quickened my step as we whirled around the compound, shoving in questions in the brief pauses of Bill's commentary.

We walked through offices, the mailroom, kitchen, dining hall, visitation area, medical rooms, warehouse, recreation room, maintenance shop, classrooms, greenhouse, and solitary confinement cells. We passed control rooms that opened and closed heavy sliding metal doors. We walked through the dorm rooms, the day rooms, the weight rooms. We passed the barbers, the cooks, the janitors, the students, the laundry workers, the yard workers, the correctional officers, the program staff, the nurses, the doctors, and the administrators.

I took deep breaths as we traveled across the vast expanse of the prison. Think of it as one big group home for eight hundred men, I told myself. Through it all, I plastered on a smile like aluminum siding and prayed that no one would guess that my heart was racing. But they did notice me, and it seemed their eyes locked on my chest. As a fifty-year-old woman whose clothes could only be described as ministerially modest, I was surprised. Everywhere else I'd passed into older age invisibility.

"Guess you're noticing that they're staring at you today," Bill observed. "It happens to any new female who walks through here. Don't be afraid."

I wasn't afraid. I was more afraid I might get the job.

Staying Fine

The tour ended at the chapel. It was a welcome oasis of quiet. We walked through the blue-carpeted sanctuary that was rather spare—only a piano and eighty chairs, and no religious symbols. Bill ushered me into his office, offering me the armchair in front of his desk, and asked why I was interested in being a chaplain.

I told him I didn't know. "I always thought that I'd be pastoring a church," I confessed, "but that isn't working out right now. I can say that I've learned to pay attention to unlikely invitations. The Spirit moves in mischievous ways, so I have to allow that it could be a nudge of the holy kind. Honestly, I might have imagined chaplaincy in a women's prison, not here."

Bill laughed. "Oh, you'll have plenty of times wishing you weren't in a men's prison. Not long ago there were two women volunteers leading a worship service and one of the inmates was fooling around with himself in the back of the chapel. I had him locked up before the women knew what was going on. So how would you handle that situation?"

Without hesitation, I said, "I wouldn't handle it at all. I'd let someone else handle it."

"You'll do just fine," said Bill.

I asked him how he stayed "fine" here.

He paused for the first time and moved his chair back. He glanced through the long, thin sliver of a window before answering. "You want to know the truth? I don't stay fine. I grew up with an alcoholic daddy. I know what it's like to be abused, what it does to your insides. I know what a lot of these guys are up against. Don't let their tough outside fool you. We all hurt." He told me that he sometimes had a tough time with the administration and the inane policies that don't "get any of us closer to safety or security or rehabilitation of lives."

"For years I've heard volunteers come into prisons and look at the inmates and say, 'There but for the grace of God go I.' Well, why would God give you the grace to avoid a hellhole like this but withhold it from these guys?" he asked. After a long pause, he added, "I have a terrific wife who loves me even when I'm not fine, and four kids whom I adore. And all of that gets me through to 'fine.'"

He leaned his forearms on the large white calendar on his desk. Except for a few neatly stacked papers, his desk was open and clear. *Open and clear.* That was a good description of my first impression of Bill. His desk appeared to be new, with the exception of gouge marks along the strip of laminated wood that faced me. Months passed before I noticed inmates sitting in that same chair pressing their pens into the wood, leaving hieroglyphics of anxiety and nervous energy.

Bill suddenly bolted out of his chair and opened the door, yelling across the chapel room to some inmates he had spied. "Hey, guys, come meet our new chaplain."

"New chaplain?" I asked.

"Okay," Bill said as he bounced back into his chair. "*Maybe*-new chaplain."

Two inmates walked into the office. We shook hands. As they leaned against the file cabinets, Bill introduced me to his clerks, Matt and Patrick.

"I don't think Matt would mind me telling you that he's been in prison over twenty years and doesn't have one infraction," said Bill. "That's quite an accomplishment. That's like never jaywalking or spitting gum on the sidewalk or anything. And Patrick's got eight down and eight to go." Bill explained that the clerks cleaned the offices and the chapel, and also kept attendance records.

Bill told them that I might be joining the chaplaincy team. "You got any questions you want to ask her?"

Matt, a short, middle-aged man with a full head of grey hair, jumped right in. "Do you have thick skin? Most of the guys will treat you with respect, but some of them will test you every chance they get. What're you going to do if one of them asks for a phone call home because they haven't heard from their family in six months and you say 'no' and then they say, 'You're the worst chaplain in the state.' Can you handle that?"

"Well," I said, "I've been called the 'anti-Christ' and the 'whore of Babylon.' And that was from Christians. So that sounds comparatively mild."

They responded with a look of surprise and one of them said, "I'll bet there's a story there."

On the Edge of Sane

We chatted a while longer. I asked the clerks what was the hardest thing about prison life. Matt said, "Some of the jerks you have to live with every day. And the food. Terrible."

Patrick nodded his head. "Yeah, the food stinks. We live on snacks from the canteen a lot of the time."

After they left, I asked Bill what kept him in there.

"I guess I'd say that being with these inmates, hearing their stories, and participating in their lives led me to look further into the mystery of life and the mercy of God," he said. "I try to help them experience God's forgiveness, and whenever possible to make amends to the people they've harmed. I've discovered that we're all loved by God irrespective of our worthiness. And if that really takes hold in you, that'll change you. For me it's been the true liberation of the Spirit."

I thanked him for his time. As I stood to leave, I saw a guitar propped up in the corner. "You play that?"

"Oh, I pick at it. Music keeps me on the edge of sane."

Back in my car, I slowly made my way past the flat, grey buildings ringed in razor coils. They looked like giant Slinkys in the fading light. I drove back home over the same mountain roads, but they seemed different. The crescent-shaped hills and evergreens were expansive and welcoming. My mind was twisting around with the curves—what it would be like to live in a world of confinement for twenty or thirty or forty years? How do you live knowing you've raped, or abused, or murdered? How could I offer a word of hope or redemption to those most despised and to men I wasn't so sure about myself?

On that long drive home, I was convinced that I couldn't possibly work in that environment. I couldn't think of anything I could offer there. I was glad to meet a person like Bill with a heart for such a ministry, but it clearly was not for me.

That night as my husband Ken prepared supper, I leaned against the kitchen counter and recounted the day. He handed me salad bowls for the table and asked the obvious. "It sounds like this chaplain wants to hire you. So what are you going to do?"

"Say no. I can't do that. I can't imagine how to be a chaplain in a men's prison."

With head tilted and eyebrows raised, Ken gave me that revealing and silent spousal look of incredulity. He knew. This story was not over yet.

The next day I received an email from Bill. He said he hoped his questions didn't scare me off. "Yesterday seemed like your first day on the job," he wrote. He said he thought I had something to offer at the prison and that he didn't need to check my references. "Whatever else I have to tell you," he added, "if your heart is sensitive, be prepared to hurt when you come to work here. You keep this place in your prayers and thoughts. You are in mine. It will be interesting to see how this changes not only the inmates' lives, but our own as well. And as Wendell Berry says, practice resurrection."

Resurrection. I was longing for it. Was it obvious? Though it was odd to think it, I had to concede that inside those grey, ugly buildings might be the place for mine.

2

Into the Glorious Debris

*Go forward with curiosity, wondering where this
experiment will lead.*

—Pema Chödrön

My training began with a review of inmate files so I'd
know our "congregation": drug dealers, drug addicts, murderers, thieves, child abusers, rapists, assaulters, etc. "And those are
just the Baptists," said our eighty-one-year-old chaplain, Bob,
with a deadpan face. He was a retired Baptist missionary and
part-time chaplain. I liked him instantly.

"Try to keep in mind," Chap Bill continued, "that inmates
are human beings just like the rest of us. We all can do terrible things, and there's always that side of ourselves we keep
hidden. If you feel overwhelmed by what they've done, try
to remember that these men are more than the crimes they
committed."

Bob slowly, deliberately, with each word wrapped in a
pause, added, "You see, we hold up a mirror to the men so

they can look at themselves. They have to learn to take respon-sibility for their actions, make amends. And you can't do this work without God. Forgiveness. Mercy. Love. That's what God is all about, so that's what we're all about."

"And sometimes the guys act like knuckleheads," Bill chimed in. "So you gotta knock 'em upside the head a few times to get through to 'em. But God's in that too."

Victor

The phone rang. It was news of a death in the family of one of the inmates. When Victor came into the office, his gen-tle face seemed stricken—being summoned to the chaplain's office was rarely a good sign. He sat down and clasped his hands tightly, waiting.

Bill broke the bad news that his grandmother had died. Victor said nothing. Then he straightened his arms. His head dropped back, heavy as a bowling ball. A soft moan unleashed a flood of tears. Bill scooted his chair over and knocked Vic-tor's knee with a balled-up hand. "You gonna be okay?" Victor nodded. "No, you're not, at least for a while you're not gonna be okay. And that's okay."

Victor told us that his grandmother raised him and he'd broken her heart when he went to prison. I reached for the box of tissues for him as tears fell. After a phone call to his family, Victor was ready to go back to his housing unit. Bill stood, put a hand on his shoulder and assured him that he could request to see a chaplain anytime.

After Victor left, I asked about his crime. "You don't want to know, but I'll tell you," Bill said. "He dropped off his son at the elementary school one morning, went home, and stabbed his wife. He's in for assault."

Albert

Bill got his guitar and started picking. A few minutes later the kitchen staff called to say that they were sending up an inmate who was "desperate" to see a chaplain. Albert was still in his white kitchen uniform when he showed up. He sat in his chair, then jumped up and looked behind him. He looked under his chair. He looked up at the ceiling.

Albert said that Satan was after him, that he saw him in the kitchen. He wanted us to perform an exorcism. "I have a demon. A sexual demon. I want these urges to stop," he pleaded. "I want Jesus to stop them. I believe in Jesus. I do. Help me! Satan's after me. Please help me!"

His face twitched and his legs jumped as he spoke. Bill pulled his chair up and cupped Albert's arm, whispering for him to calm down. "Albert, you don't have a demon. You're struggling with your sexuality. We can help with that, but not with an exorcism." Albert persisted, shaking his head and yelling that Satan had him. Then he screamed out "Jesus! Jesus!"

Albert was escorted to the psychologist's office. I was ready to jump out of my chair and leave. I wasn't trained in mental health and had no idea how to handle someone like Albert. Such an incident was rare, Bill assured me, and said he couldn't believe it happened on my first day. "Don't worry," he said. "You'll be fine." I wasn't so sure. He said time would tell whether the inmate was "faking" craziness in order to go back to Central, his preferred prison, or whether he really had serious mental problems. "But this much we know. He's HIV-positive, infecting guys on his housing unit. That has to stop."

Jesus.

The day was only half over. I was exhausted. I went to my office and busied myself with arranging a few things. Some books on the shelf, a calendar on the wall, some pens on the desk. No, not pens on the desk. That could be a weapon, I thought. I put them in my drawer. But who was I kidding? If someone wanted to kill me they could do it with their bare hands. What in the world did I think I was doing there? I wondered if I was the delusional one.

A Brief Prison Primer

Bill and I were going over the upcoming services when two officers stopped by. They were being cordial enough but clearly sizing me up as a newbie. "Not everyone is cut out for this work, you know," the sergeant offered. "High stress. High divorce rate. Plenty of heart attacks. In here you gotta be the same every single day."

"Are you divorced?" I asked.

"Yeah," he said flatly. Then he returned to my lesson. "These inmates will turn on you at any time. Don't ever trust 'em. Ever. If I come in here, young lady, and tell you to leave, you leave. No questions asked. Trouble can happen in a second. If you and I get stuck behind a slide* with an inmate, they'll do the same thing to me as they will to you, only you're built for it."

He didn't have to explain what he meant. Whether they were "warning" or "teaching" me, whether they were an inmate or an officer, in time I could see that they both indulged in their own fantasies at my expense.

"I'm from the old school," he continued. "I've been around a long time. I liked things better when we could settle problems the old way around here." He punched his fist into the palm of his hand. "The men can understand this."

It was becoming a bad Western movie. I wanted to ride off into the sunset, but the lecture wasn't over.

---

* A sliding door, managed by officers from a Master Control room.

Tell Her the Truth

"Now we've got all these new rules. 'Course some of 'em are good for us. But I can tell you when I started out, you could've walked across this camp and been jumped, assaulted, and raped." "Sarge," Bill said, "I've been around a long time too. That never happened. Besides, as chaplains we have a different relationship with the inmates, and most of them respect us."

The sergeant kept his laser glare on me, telling me how you can't trust "any of 'em" and you have to treat inmates like inmates. "Tell her," he said to Bill. "Tell her the truth."

"Truth is I've been such a sorry bastard in my life that I just don't have room to judge," Bill replied.

Undeterred, the sergeant kept on. "Yeah, well, I've seen more than you. If I was in charge of the prisons, I'd bring back chain gangs, chain 'em together to pick up trash on the highways. I'd have 'em digging ditches with pick axes."

Sarge also didn't believe they should have TV or phone privileges, the weights or rec room, earn money or have "all these damn programs." Didn't believe in medical or dental care either. "If a tooth is bad, pull it out. We're too soft on these guys. Let their families pay for their food and their medical bills." He believed that the moment someone committed a crime, most of their rights had been forfeited.

"Our prisons have become a piece of cake," he said. "It's too easy here. They get everything. I'd make it so miserable that they'd never want to come back. Fear is the only language they understand. Let 'em know they can't get away with their sorry, lazy behavior. Make 'em scared of you. That's how to get respect." His assessment of the death penalty was that it was the right solution in the wrong place, that it needed to be in the middle of town, within sight of everyone, so everyone could "see the guy hanging from a noose."

and hire new staff for the Baptist Peace Fellowship of North America, for which he was the founding executive director. Our shy younger daughter started high school and struggled to find her place. Our older daughter went off to college. We were hemorrhaging financially.

I scrambled to find work anywhere, speaking at conferences, in churches, at retreats. A tiny mountain church with twenty people welcomed me as their interim pastor. A house church in Boone invited me to lead their group once a month. But the financial woes were still overwhelming. I exchanged one set of struggles for another. I inflicted heartache on my family. Far from a new door opening when one has closed, I discovered that a dozen more may slam shut in front of you.

After all I'd been through, after all I'd imagined my life to be, it would be God's holy joke if prison was the place for me to be restored. Given the narrowing confines of my internal landscape, I had to admit I was "pitched and wrecked" as Barbara Kingsolver says in *High Tide in Tucson*. Every one of us, she wrote, has to start our lives anew at some point—for some of us at many points:

> And onward full tilt we go, pitched and wrecked and absurdly resolute, driven in spite of everything to make good on a new shore. To be hopeful, to embrace one possibility after another—that is surely the basic instinct. . . . Time to move out into the glorious debris. Time to take this life for what it is.

I began to think about how, in spite of everything, I might make good on a new shore. And surely I'd found the most glorious debris.

3

Learning to Count

Not everything that can be counted counts,
and not everything that counts can be counted.

—William Bruce Cameron

Employee training was in one of the maximum security prisons. I was in a class with twenty-seven new correctional officers, most of them twenty-somethings. The program director clarified things right up front: "You may have heard that program people are inmate advocates. Let me assure you that we are not. We did not ask them to come here. We take them where they are and do what we can to get them ready to move on."

We learned about conflict management, communication skills, fire safety, and communicable diseases. One morning's session was on sexual harassment. The women and men were divided into separate groups and asked to make a list of what we found offensive as well as acceptable about the other gender.

I stayed quiet but the other seven women came up with a list of offensive behaviors that included when men grab themselves in the crotch, spit their tobacco into a cup and leave it there, make body noises, finger-blow their noses, and make comments about our body parts. The acceptable list of behaviors was when the men smell good, buy us candy bars, treat us like a lady, and are nice with no strings attached.

The men's offensive-behavior list for women included complaining too much, being too emotional, having something to prove, gossiping too much, letting our emotions rule, and getting "all riled up" about things. What they liked about women was our different perspective, our ability to understand, and our courage working in a hostile environment.

The men and women reacted to each other's list with nervous laughter.

Peppered Language

The last afternoon was the dreaded pepper spray training. In order to carry pepper spray, you had to be sprayed yourself. It was an application of the Golden Rule with a twist: don't do unto others what you wouldn't want done unto you.

Unlike the others, I was not required to carry the small metal container of pepper spray, but as the oldest one in the group, and the only chaplain, I thought I shouldn't be exempt from the group trauma experience. Solidarity, you know.

As we were heading outside to be sprayed, a half dozen young male officers said some version of "Chap, forgive me if I yell something bad in front of you. I don't mean to offend you." I assured them that I wasn't taking names and was fairly certain I'd let a few words fly myself.

We lined up four at a time. I stepped up, said my name, and was "shot" across my eyes. It stung like crazy. Blindly, I was escorted by a nurse to a water hose and was told to keep my eyes open for a blast of cleansing water and baby shampoo. Then I was placed in front of a giant fan to soothe the burning skin. The worst was over in twenty minutes, but that sunburned feeling lasted for hours.

As predicted, there was yelling and cussing throughout the whole ordeal, but who cared? It only added to the feeling of solidarity. And we all passed the test; we could all be issued pepper spray. Being the nonviolent type, I wondered if I'd ever want to use it. Still, I was glad I had gone through the exercise with my fellow workers.

Solitary

The last part of the day was a tour of the maximum security prison where the day's training had taken place. About ten of us were escorted through the halls, the housing units, and up the stairs to the solitary confinement cells—"segregation," or "seg." There were 116 seg cells.

The men peered through the six-inch-wide windows that ran the length of the seg doors, down to a small trap that opened for food, letters, magazines, or meds. When they saw us, they whistled loudly and yelled obscenities. As they banged on the thick metal doors, the unit manager explained that it was a self-sufficient unit where all the needs of the inmates were met. They were given fifteen minutes a day for a shower, plus thirty to forty-five minutes a day of walking, either outside in a fenced cell or inside in front of their cells.

I'd seen solitary confinement on television, of course, but I wasn't prepared for my visceral reaction to such a bleak place, all concrete and steel. Seeing so many faces peering out of narrow windowpanes, I told myself to breathe deeply and walk steadily. I'll never get over seeing this, I thought. Maybe I never should.

When the tour of the maximum security prison was completed, I was relieved that I didn't work there. I thanked God

Even so, I was surprised when the administration asked me to offer a prayer for the dedication of the new firing range. *A firing range?* I wasn't sure I could do that. A place where people are trained to kill other people?

Then again I wondered if I'd already crossed the ethical line back when I was in Memphis. I was asked to pray over a preseason NFL game, and I had a little crisis of conscience about it. Why pray at a football game? Did God care? Wasn't God more into baseball?

I had told Ken I was wrestling with the decision. "Are they giving you tickets?" he asked.

"Skybox."

"You should definitely pray," he said without hesitation.

So I had found a way to pray at a football game for the greater good (of my marriage). But this firing range request seemed a real conflict of interest. Target practice for the correctional officers consisted of aiming at a drawing of a man wearing a prison uniform. I wondered what kind of celebratory prayer I could offer for a thing like that. I lost sleep puzzling over it. Again, I sought advice from Ken.

"Go ahead and do it," he said. "No one listens to public prayers anyway."

So out on the field that day, enfolded by the surrounding hills and whispering pines, I prayed what words I could believe: *Thank you, God, for your sustaining presence everywhere. . . . even here, even now. May you watch over everyone who comes to these grounds. Protect them and keep them safe. May we remember that you are watching all we do. . . even here, even now. Keep in close range as we aim for the day when we don't need a place like this. And may we always be within range of your hope for this old broken world, where one day we can all live unafraid and in peace with each other. Amen.*

My husband was right—no one listened. They went straight for the soda and cookies, talking of football.

Compassion vs. Custody

It's not my practice to question conversion experiences, but it was noticeable that some guys got the urge to be Muslim around the time of the feast that comes at the end of Ramadan fasting. And who wouldn't want such a spread? The prayer leader's mother brought in chicken, fried flounder, lamb, macaroni and cheese, potato salad, turnips, greens, white rice, shrimp stir-fry, pinto beans, couscous, yeast rolls, biscuits, chocolate cake, and banana pudding. After she delivered the coolers of food, I escorted her back to the gate. "I'm sorry you can't stay, Mrs. Aboud. I'm not sure why they won't allow it. I know the men would like to thank you for all this beautiful food."

We passed the officer in charge who asked where we were going and then said, "Come see me on your way back, Chap."

I thanked Mrs. Aboud, and we said our goodbyes. Then the officer called out, "Who was that?"

I explained it was the prayer leader's mother who brought the food.

"She wasn't authorized to be here, and if the superintendent knew, he would have my hide and yours, too."

"Yes. All right."

"Whose mother is she?"

I pointed to Sameh.

"Don't point!" he scolded.

I explained that she only brought the food; she wasn't staying.

"You don't let anyone into this prison that hasn't been authorized!" he shouted. "I don't care if it's the pope or Jimmy Swaggart, you don't let them in. Do you understand me?"

"Yes. It won't happen again. And I'm with you on not letting Jimmy Swaggart in here."

"Let me tell you something, Chap," he said, calmly but

directly. "I think compassion is good sometimes. I like to be compassionate. But I am not compassion. You are compassion, and I am custody. . . and custody must be in control. Custody wins. Do you understand that?"

"Yes," I said, as compassionately as I could.

Speaking of Food

For another religious feast, one group of inmates decided to collect enough money to order thirty-five pizzas, one large pizza for *each* person. After prayers of thanksgiving, the long-anticipated meal was devoured with glee. All too soon the festive time of eating ended.

"Sorry, guys," I reminded them in what I was afraid was an old schoolmarm voice. "You know custody won't allow the leftovers to leave the room with you."

Frowning, they hurried another box around the tables for final bites, but even so, three pizzas remained. While I was pondering whether to take them home or leave them for officers, a sergeant, totally oblivious to the pizza dilemma, started talking to me about a letter she intercepted. She said it implied all kinds of "vulgar stuff" allegedly going on in my office. She didn't want "a lady as nice" as me to see the letter but wanted to let me know.

By then the men were filing out, and some were still being patted down. When I went to the table to get the leftover pizza, it was all gone. I asked my clerk where it went. He offered no explanation beyond the recognizable stare of *you-don't-want-to-know*.

It gave new meaning to the words "stuffed pizza"; they simply put slices down the front of their pants. Needless to say, it was quite a while before I ate pizza again.

The Dumb Game

Probably the hardest thing for me to master was when "undue familiarity" collided with common human decency. One of the inmate clerks said he was "feeling woozy." He was on a new medication and said the doctor had told him that if he felt dizzy to report it to medical immediately. So I called the nurse and was told that only the inmate could make the request. Within a few minutes my supervisor called to tell me that chaplain clerks don't get special treatment. "Don't call medical. The inmates can put in their own request." For a fleeting moment, I thought I should explain it was kind of an emergency—but "emergency" in that place apparently fell under different rules. I said I understood, though I didn't.

We almost lost one of our clerks over underwear. "I think I might lose my job, Chap," he announced one morning. "They searched my cell and found extra pairs of underwear. One of them was raggedy and I used washable markers to draw on it. They wrote me up for destroying state property."

At first I was baffled by these kinds of incidents, but I slowly started figuring out "prison think." When the copy machine got a paper jam, maintenance came to fix it. Our clerk knew what the problem was and offered the solution to the staff worker. Sure enough, the jam was fixed. Once the maintenance worker was gone, I cautioned our clerk, "Don't ever talk to a staff member that way."

Surprised, he asked, "What way?"

"Like you're a real human being. You can't offer advice to a staff member unless they ask you. They'll think you're acting out of place, like you're being uppity or something. You could lose your job. You could be written up for disrespecting staff. You could end up in seg with an infraction and then sent to another prison."

"Okay, Chap. I know how to play dumb."

"I hate that game, but it's how you play smart in here," I said.

I don't think I'd have been brave enough to stay if it hadn't been for Chap Bill. I took courage from his strength and optimism. I soaked in his way of staying just inside the rules while still demonstrating a modicum of mercy and humor. And there were inmates and officers, too, who could unexpectedly touch my heart and bring me up short.

One inmate with learning disabilities told me how proud he was that there was just one more week to go before finishing his class called "Thinking for a Change."

"Chap, I'm really thinking for a change." That's good, I told him, thinking is good.

"I'm taking all the classes I can. It will take five years off my sentence."

"How long is your sentence?"

"110 years."

4

Below Good

*We can never know what is in the heart of
another until we can find it in our own.*

— Robert Koehler

Over time, my name was on a growing file of missteps,
confirming what some said all along: I had no business being
there. That was especially true at the maximum security prison
when I was hired to be head chaplain. One of my worst mis-
takes started with a turkey sandwich. I brought food for the
program staff lunch, only to learn it was postponed. With more
sandwiches than I could eat, I spread the fixings on my desk
and invited the clerks to have at it. Didn't seem like much to
me, but for them it would be a gourmet meal.

I knew better. We weren't allowed to give anything to an
inmate. There were good reasons for the policy, but at the time
I couldn't remember them.

The clerks were eyeing the food when suddenly two officers
walked into my office—a lieutenant and a DHO—disciplinary

hearing officer. It was their annual visit to all program staff to question our knowledge of disciplinary procedures. If timing is everything, mine was impeccable.

The inmates quickly left my office, but the incriminating evidence remained on my desk. I asked the officers if they'd like a sandwich. No takers. The DHO asked his rapid-fire questions. Did I know what to do if a disturbance broke out with inmates? Yes, I would call custody. Did I know which form to fill out for writing up a statement on an incident? Yes. What is the title on the form? I couldn't remember. The DHO officer scribbled some words on his evaluation sheet. "We're finished." My churning gut thought he said, "You're finished."

The lieutenant asked, "And what about these sandwiches? Who are they for?"

I confessed. Yes, I'd offered them to the clerks, but they didn't touch them.

"But you know the rules." Yes. I knew the rules.

The officers walked to the front of the chapel to ask the clerks to step out of their cubicle. Everyone knew the routine. The men turned around with their hands behind their backs to be handcuffed. Silent and helpless, I stood watching from the other side of the chapel. Any type of intervention on my part would have made everything worse for all of us. Not expecting to see me again, one of the clerks said as he passed through the chapel door, "Peace to you, Chap."

Peace. There was none of it within or around me. I wanted to lock the chapel door, hide in my office, and cry. But there was no time for that. I had to buck up and go see my boss before he got the news secondhand.

I went out the chapel door and caught a glimpse of the clerks as they were escorted down the stairs to seg at the opposite end of the prison. I walked alone with leaden feet and a racing heart to my supervisor's office to submit my resignation.

As I spilled out my wrongdoings, I also made a plea for the clerks. I knew that they could lose their jobs and their hard-earned efforts to maintain an infraction-free prison record.

"I was wrong to offer the sandwiches, but the clerks didn't eat them." My boss said that we'd all be placed under internal investigation.

Driving home from work, my mind replayed the scene of the two clerks being handcuffed and led away. I was the cause. My body desperately tried to purge the day. The usual forty-five minute drive home took longer, interrupted by three stops on the side of the highway to heave. I was anxious to be home, but Ken was out of town. He wasn't available with his listening ear and reassuring hugs. I decided to stop by the home of close friends. They invited me to their back porch, shaded by an expansive willow tree. I sank into the wide arms of a porch rocker and told the whole story.

"I was three years at the medium security prison. It looks like I won't make it three months at the maximum unit," I concluded.

"What?" My friends were incredulous. "You mean you could lose your job over turkey sandwiches?" They gave me a bowl of hot soup and a glass of wine. The "peace" the clerk blessed me with was beginning to seep in. But for the clerks in solitary, there would be no such sanctuary among willows, or comfort food from friends.

Hold the Mayo

The next day at work it seemed that people were looking at a scarlet letter on my forehead. The prison rumor mill was in full swing, churning out a far more salacious scenario about what happened with the new female chaplain and her clerks.

After three days I was summoned for my interrogation. Three staff members sat at one end of a long conference table while I sat at the other end in the lower regions of hell. The questioning commenced.

"Was there mayonnaise on the desk?"

"No. Mustard. Brown."

"Was there lettuce on the desk?"

"Yes. Romaine."

"Was the bread in a bag or on a plate?"

"In a bag. Plastic."

"Was the turkey in a sandwich or on a plate?"

"On a plate. Paper."

"Did you offer turkey sandwiches to the chaplain clerks?"

"Yes, I did."

I was sent from the room while the investigating team deliberated. Ten minutes passed before I received the verdict.

"Chaplain Sehested, you won't be fired, but you have been charged with 'bad judgment' and 'undue familiarity.' You will be given a 'BG' on your record."

BG? I'd never heard of that. The only association that came to mind was "Bad Girl." Were they charging me with being a bad girl? I could hardly wait to tell my husband.

"And what exactly does 'BG' stand for?" I asked.

"Below Good. Sign your name just below the charge."

"And the clerks? What about them?"

"They will be released from seg and reinstated in their jobs in the chaplaincy office."

It was a miracle. I'd expected them to be sent to another prison on the next available bus. They, too, received a charge of "undue familiarity," an infraction on their record, and one week in seg.

As I left the prison, I walked down the stairs with an uncommon bounce of release. It was good that we all kept our jobs, of course, but it was more than that. I wanted to run up to anyone and everyone to tell them that I was "Below Good." As a life-long overachiever, I felt a measure of relief having my below-goodness a matter of public record. The truth was out. I was BG, too.

When I reached the lobby, one of the administrators was standing there waiting for me. He stopped me before I reached the door and said, "Chaplain, I'm sorry we did that to you, but we had to let you know where you are."

"Yes, thank you," I replied. "I do believe I know just where I am."

Backs against the Wall

During the Montgomery bus boycott, Martin Luther King Jr. kept a book with him called *Jesus and the Disinherited*. Written by famed theologian Howard Thurman, the book was published in 1949 and became a foundation for the civil rights movement. In this thin volume, Thurman took up the question of what Jesus's teachings had to say to "those who stand, at a moment in human history, with their backs against the wall." Nowhere was that so relevant, literally and figuratively, than in my prison work. Days could be tedious and frustrating, but the larger question always loomed of how to minister to what society thinks of the worst people, how to keep the spirit alive under the circumstances, how to let the teachings of Jesus make some kind of difference in what I felt, what I taught, what I witnessed.

What I wasn't prepared for was a bitter pill to take—what I was truly up against. I was living in massive institutionalized racism.

I still get a chill when I remember the time I passed two inmates cleaning the floors. An officer called them to another part of the

The Writing Group

The writer William S. Burroughs wrote about getting drunk one night and thinking he could shoot a glass off the top of his wife's head, but missed it and killed her instead. He wrote that the horror of it brought in "the invader, the Ugly Spirit," resulting in "a lifelong struggle in which I have had no choice but to write my way out." I thought that maybe I could help some of the inmates write their way out, too. But I knew I would need help.

A volunteer leader for the weekly writing group was known to the guys as "Monk" even though he was far from being a solemn monkish man. His gently swinging arms could circle into a bear hug with ease, something that was good medicine for the men, even though hugs were forbidden. Monk was a life-long rebel against heartlessness in a way that embodied both maverick and mystic. A retired Baptist pastor, a grandfather, a potter, and a banjo player, Monk had been a mentor to me for over twenty-five years.

Although we weren't trained to lead a writing group, we loved words, and we knew writing could clear personal thickets to pathways toward revelation and healing.

Our sessions began with silence, prayer, and a reading. Then the men shared their writing assignments, covering topics like forgiveness, a lost childhood, or what it was like to have birthdays in prison year after year.

Beyond Good

A twenty-three-year-old with a life sentence asked to join the group, saying simply, "I wanna be a writer." Usually that was reason enough for me, though I did question his gang affiliation—that he didn't deny. "It's the best family I've ever had," he said honestly.

"Ok then," I said. "How should I introduce you? What's the name you like to go by?"

"BG." I asked him what that stood for, but he said he couldn't tell me.

"Guess I'll just say it means 'Beyond Good,'" I told him.

As the guys were gathering for the writing group, I introduced them to BG, and then gave them an assignment to take the next thirty minutes to write about the best thing they'd ever done. BG was the last to read his story that night.

He was just sixteen years old when he was a new dad trying to help his baby son survive. Sitting on apartment steps in the predawn hours, he sold small bags of heroin, the morning hit for addicts. One morning BG saw an elderly woman coming down the sidewalk, bending and picking something up. When she got in front of him, he asked what she was doing.

"Picking up coins. It's my tithe to my church. In a good month, I find about twenty dollars."

He thought that was a good thing. So he reached in his pocket and pulled out two hundred dollars' worth of bills. "Here, lady. Take this."

She refused. "No, son. I don't want that kind of money. I'll do it my way. God bless you."

BG was upset that she wouldn't take his money. But a week later he arrived on the streets early. Up and down the sidewalk, he dropped four hundred dollars in nickels, dimes, and quarters. Then he sat and waited. Through the morning fog, she appeared as usual, bending and gathering. When she got in front of him, she stopped and smiled. He smiled. Then she turned and walked on down the street.

BG finished reading his story, and the room erupted. All the guys jumped up, yelling and slapping him on the back, repeating over and over, "That's beyond good!" "That's beyond good, man!"

AN UNUSUAL FLOCK

5

All-purpose Chaplain

Never be angry with your neighbor because
his religious views differ from your own;
for all the branches of a tree do not lean the same way.

—William Scott Downey, *Proverbs* (1851)

I was a little surprised that we had Wiccans. For one thing, I thought they were only female. But an inmate named Jackson, a fairly new Wiccan, came in hopping mad one day and said he needed to take somebody out. "I can't take it, Chap. You don't know what it's like on the unit. I'm going to have to slug somebody."

"Really, Jackson?" I tried to get him to look me in the eye. "How about me? Wanna take a slug at me?"

He covered his face with his hands and let out a bearish *uhhh*.

"You know, Jackson," I said softly to him, "you may be the only Wiccan some people ever meet. I think you should think about that, and just be the best Wiccan you can be."

41

Jackson took a peppermint from my candy jar, so I did too, and we let our sacramental candies melt in our mouths. After a few minutes, he got up and just said, "Okay."

I opened another peppermint and thought about his visit. When I was in seminary, I never imagined a day that I'd tell someone to "just be the best Wiccan you can be."

Jackson managed to push through his anger, and good conversations followed as we found strategies for him to use when that anger had no place to go. Not all the Wiccans were so fond of me. One day an inmate stopped by to say a Wiccan put a curse on me. "That's why you're looking so old, Chap."

"I'm looking old because I've been putting up with you guys," I said.

Sacred Rabbit Foot

I can't say I knew a lot about what prison chaplains did. I assumed it involved some preaching, organizing Bible studies, giving pastoral advice. You see chaplains in movies, usually priests, walking with the condemned, or giving last rites. Occasionally, there might be a jailhouse confession needed for a plot twist. My dad was a chaplain in World War II, but he didn't talk much about it. He brought back a German Bible with the book of Esther ripped out by the Nazis—apparently, they didn't want Queen Esther's defiance of authority to inspire anyone.

I knew the prison would have Protestants, Catholics, maybe a few Jews, likely very few, since it was North Carolina. I figured there'd be a Buddhist or two, probably a few Muslims. And I knew that the Christians likely would be more traditional than my own practice. So I was surprised to discover there were a dozen religious groups approved for program and worship in the state prisons: Asatru, Assemblies of Yahweh,

Native American, Buddhist, Christian, Hindu, Muslim, Moorish Science Temple, Jew, Messianic Jew, Rastafarian, and Wiccan. When I asked if interest was expressed in any other religions, a few inmates said they practiced Satanism, yet another kind of worship I didn't know much about.

There were a few Asatrus but none who grew up practicing the religion. Their nine noble virtues were easy enough to encourage: courage, truth, honor, fidelity, discipline, hospitality, industriousness, perseverance, and self-reliance. These were gleaned from the ancient Poetic Edda, as well as the Icelandic Sagas and Germanic folklore. I imagined the Asatrus as a band of Vikings crossing the stormy seas with camaraderie and courage. Unfortunately, our group often became a haven for the white supremacists instead.

A sergeant from one of the housing units called one day and said, "I got a Buddhist inmate down here who says that he can keep his rabbit's foot because it's a sacred object in his religion. That true?"

I told him it may be sacred to the inmate, but it was not a requirement of the Buddhist faith to keep a rabbit's foot.

Saying Your Prayers

A little-known version of Islam is the Moorish Science Temple of America (M.S.T. of A.). It was founded in 1913 in Newark, New Jersey, by Timothy Drew, known as Prophet Noble Drew Ali. He held the belief that African Americans are descendants of the Moors of Northwest Africa, making them Moorish by nationality and Islamic by faith.

During supper in the chow hall one night, officers spotted four inmates with their hands raised, two fingers held up on one hand, all five on the other. Assuming gang-related signs were being passed, the officers handcuffed the inmates and led them away for questioning. During the interrogation, they all insisted that they were praying.

The special affairs captain called me in. I asked him if the men were all members of the Moorish Science Temple faith, and he confirmed that they were.

"That's one reason we're checking them out. We shut down that group last year for gang activity."

"If they held up five fingers on their left hand, it's symbolic of love, truth, peace, freedom, and justice," I said. "Two fingers on the right hand stand for Allah and humanity. They likely were saying grace."

"Still could be gang signs. We'll tell 'em they gotta pray silently like everybody else."

Don't Ask the Name

The Rastafarians made it clear that I wasn't a very good chaplain. Policy would come down from state, about things like the length of their dreadlocks or approved colors for their prayer crowns, as they were called. They were sure I was behind it. One time they sat stone-faced and furious in their "reasoning circle" because I was ten minutes late in calling them in and "all the other groups" were called on time.

"Chap, if we were in your place, we'd be advocating for the group hard."

I laughed. "If you were in my place, you'd be looking for another job."

But I did try to go the extra mile for them and get a concert approved, especially after I'd heard about a reggae band that was "devoted to love, justice, and the evolution of spiritual principles." Sounded good to me.

I waited until I thought my boss was in a good mood. Or to be clear, in a good mood with me since it seemed I was always doing something wrong. One time he did actually apologize for yelling at me. "I brought something with me this morning that I should've left at the gate," he explained. I was gobsmacked.

I made my request for a concert.

Bossman: "What's the name of the band?"

Me: "I can't tell you."

Bossman: "Tell me."

Me: "Ok, but don't say no because of their name. It's the Black Rebels."

Bossman: (throwing up his hands): "*Are you kidding me? Don't you know there's racial tension in this place?*"

Me: "We don't have to use their name."

Bossman: "Okay. No name. And no trouble. Anything happens, it's on you."

But something did happen. Two hundred inmates filled a room to hear the rhythmic and mesmerizing music of the Black Rebels. The concrete grey walls lifted to the heights of a cathedral with something rarely witnessed in so many inmates at one time: joy. The concert incited a revival of their spirits that permeated the prison with peace and goodwill for many days. Not to mention getting me a short reprieve from the Rastas.

Scott

I went to seg to see if anyone wanted a visit. An officer walked before me, yelling, "Anyone want to see a chaplain? We got one here."

One voice yelled out, "I don't want to see any goddamn chaplain."

Another guy yelled out, "You might want to see this one."

The officer yelled, "You guys shut up. If you want to see

6

That Old-time Religion

Sir, a woman's preaching is like a dog's walking on his hind legs.
It is not done well; but you are surprised to find it done at all.

—Samuel Johnson, 1763

"I thought you oughtta know," Lester informed me, clutching his Bible close to his chest, "I ain't never gonna go to any service when you're preaching 'cause you're one of the seven abominations from hell."

"One of the seven? I love that. I had no idea I was so powerful." Lester was stony faced. "But tell me. Who am I up against? Who are the other six?"

He sputtered, "I don't know. I'll have to study on it."

Roping Them In

Lester's admonition echoed what I knew others believed, but when it came time to preach my first Sunday service at the prison, Chaplain Bob, Chaplain Bill, and the inmate clerks set up all eighty chairs, anticipating the curiosity seekers.

The clerks said that they would be stationed in the middle of the outside aisles. Bill said that he and Bob would be parked at the back of the chapel. I asked why they were going to so much trouble.

"We don't want any 'public arousals' during your sermon."

I didn't tell them that I was more worried about putting my new congregation to sleep. In retrospect, I guess I did come in with a crazy idea. Chap Bill tells the story. . .

In the first place, I don't know how in the hell she got a long rope past the front gate. But true to Nancy form, right smack dab in the middle of her sermon she ties an inmate up in this rope and has the other end tied around herself. So, as she's standing up there using this elaborate prop to explain something profound about forgiveness, an officer walks into the chapel. He takes one look at Chaplain Celestial—that's what he called her since he couldn't say "Sehested"—looked at me and said, "Chap, what the hell is she doing?"

"Have you been forgiven of your sins?" I asked the officer. I was having to whisper since Chap Celestial was still preaching. "If there is someone in your life you need to forgive, it's sort of like having a rope tied around you connected to the person you need to forgive." Binding. Unbinding.

I guess that wasn't the answer to his question. "What the hell is she doing with a rope? And why is that inmate tied up? You know how many lawsuits we're looking at? How did she get a rope in here?"

"She's new here. This is her first sermon. I promise I will get the rope out of here soon as she quits preaching. And I promise I won't ever let her tie up another inmate again. Just please let this be between us. You

and I both know there's several officers here who don't
think a woman has any place in prisons. And we both
know that a whole bunch of people don't believe in
women preachers. This won't happen again. I promise.
Just don't tell any other officers or the Captain."

He assured me he wouldn't speak of this to anyone
else. As soon as the service ended, I managed to sneak
the rope out of the prison. And as far as I know, Chaplain Celestial never tied up another inmate.*

I can't claim to have won over many guys with my preaching. But I did get this ringing endorsement one Sunday during the service, when Hank confessed, "I once believed that
women couldn't preach, but then I decided that if God can
speak through Balaam's ass, then God can speak through
Chaplain Sehested."

Preach from the Heart

The guys who thought I might be an okay preacher, if
only I knew what I was doing, tried to explain it to me. "You
gotta preach from the heart," they instructed. "You'd get men
to cry and you'd see lives changed and you'd have the power
to do that."

Who said I hadn't made grown men cry?

They continued to map it out. "You should talk at the beginning of the service. You should say, 'Praise the Lord,' and then
we'll say, 'Praise the Lord,' and then you say, 'God is good,' and
we'll say, 'all the time.' And then you can ask us about our week."

It sounded like a great plan, but I just couldn't pull it off.
I have to say, though, my preaching professor was none other

---

* Bill Stewart, unpublished manuscript.

than Dr. James A. Forbes, one of the country's most renowned preachers. He wouldn't settle for my delivering a milquetoast sermon. But for the most part, the guys wanted milkshakes of happy gospel.

Even so, there were milkshake sermons—somewhat innocuous—and then there was downright rotten thinking. As for the latter, Gary was in a class by himself. When he appeared at my doorway, he was beaming. "It was God's will that I come to prison, Chap!" he blurted out. "God's got something flowing in my heart, and I just got to tell you. I want to share my story with everyone."

What I knew of Gary's "story" was that he killed his cousin's toddler. An unthinkable crime, banished to the land of things too horrific to contemplate. But Gary figured it out—first blaming his family, then the alcohol, the drugs, even the district attorney.

"God is awesome," his litany began. "God blessed me today."

I knew that some of the Christian volunteers invited him to tell his conversion story in services, and it baffled him that I didn't offer him the same invitation. Then he got to the heart of it. "You see, Chap, it was God's will that I come to prison. Everything that's happened has been in God's plan for me. I'd never have come to know God if I hadn't been sent to prison. I wish I could write my cousin and tell her everything happens for a reason. I wish I could tell her it was all God's will."

I rose up, the mother in me coming out in full force. "Never, ever, link the words 'God's will' with the death of a child. Never. You were the cause, Gary, and no one else but you—not God."

Gary's big grin left his face, and with that, he left the chapel.

True Confessions

One inmate wanted to know if I just decided to become a minister from "my own idea," or was I "anointed by the Holy Spirit?"

The truth is, I never imagined that I would seek ordination or become a pastor, even though—or because—my father and grandfather were Baptist preachers. During my first semester in seminary, I heard a woman preach for the first time. Actually that's not true. I had heard women preach all my life, but they were called missionaries, and their sermons were called "devotionals" or "testimonies." Hearing a woman named a preacher offer words called a sermon was new to me. Her presence in the pulpit changed my world. Yet after the service, I remember with regret the words I spoke to my husband. "I loved her sermon. It was like water on dry earth. I don't have any problems with women being preachers. I just don't think I'd want one for my pastor."

Looking aghast, my husband challenged, "Well, why not?"

Why not, indeed. His words jolted me, causing walls of cultural conditioning to tumble down. It was not my theology that bound me. It was deep-seated societal norms and images that held me captive. Seminary became a training ground for excising old ways of thinking to make way for new ones, ones that required imagination. Remembering my own transformation about gender roles helped me understand the resistance of others in the years that followed.

Holding a Master of Divinity degree from a highly regarded seminary was no guarantee of employment. It took three years before a lively renegade Baptist church in Decatur, Georgia, hired and ordained me. As their associate pastor, I received the kind of encouragement found in a community of compassion and courage. But no amount of support prepared me for the exhaustion in body and soul of being in pastoral leadership. After only a few years, I was ready to step out of ministry and find other work.

One evening I plopped down in my mother's kitchen chair while we prepared dinner. "Mother, I can't do it. This trying to be a wife, mother, and minister is just too hard. There is so much need all around, so many people hurting everywhere. I can't do this work. I have roving guilt. One week it falls on my family for not doing enough, and the next week it falls on the church. I feel like a failure."

My mother stopped stirring the soup, looked at me with spoon in hand and said, "Nancy, there is something deep within all of us that won't let go, no matter how many times we try to push it away. This world is a struggle. It's not easy for you, but you are doing it with all that is within you, and it is a better road than letting the something inside you die."

The "something within" stayed with me as I accepted the call to be the senior minister of a Southern Baptist church in Tennessee. It was 1987. The church was stunningly brave to call me at such a divisive time in the denomination. But even before my husband, two young daughters, and I unpacked the moving van in Memphis, my new church was in the process of being "disfellowshipped" (excommunicated) from the Southern Baptist Convention for the heresy of "knowingly calling a woman as pastor."

I swirled in the center of the controversy with equal portions of hatred and love from far-flung corners of the country. In letters to the editor, in letters to the church, in heated denominational meetings, words like "Jezebel," "whore of Babylon," and yes, "an abomination from hell" were hurled my way. I had daily opportunities to love my enemies, but it was difficult when my own heart went to war.

That October, four hundred people filled a sanctuary for the annual denominational gathering and to take action against our church. After the meeting, the lead pastor of the excommunication said to me, "I hope you didn't take this personally." I was dumbfounded. I'd listened to rants about women being the first to sin in the Garden of Eden, relegated to second-class status in the social order. I'd heard passionate cries that female pastors "violate the word of God." I knew that women like me were standing against the historical and societal gravity that wanted to keep us seated, silent, and smiling. It was impossible to barricade my spirit from all the hateful words. I told the pastor that I did take it personally because I am a person, after all, and not simply an issue.

Nothing prepared me for the sheer meanness of some Christians. But I wasn't expecting the outpouring of support I received, either. Heaven and hell can be found in the same place. I met wonderful people in the larger faith community who sent encouraging words and came to my aid with support, laughter, and diversions when I needed them most. I tried to remember the words of Helen Keller: "Although the world is full of suffering, it is full also of the overcoming of it." I sought to plant my feet firmly on the ground of the overcoming side.

For many years I continued to be on the front lines of the debate about women in ministry. I'd become a symbol, for good and ill, for the movement. Or maybe I was less a symbol than a target—a target of hatred, suspicion, and rejection by fundamentalists who, by definition, do not yield. But I was also a symbol of hope for many women who were beginning to pursue their calling in the church. That, too, takes a toll. It takes a fierce attentiveness to your own spirit to minimize confusion between you as the symbol and you as the person. Even with an extraordinary support system—a loving

scripture, hungry to find a deeper meaning. "As the hart panteth after the brook, so panteth my soul after thee, O God," as
they would say with the Psalmist.

Years ago I received a letter from an inmate who'd been in
prison for eighteen years and was serving a life sentence. He
wrote about finding that deeper meaning: *Isn't life funny? We
find joy and happiness and momentary glimpses of God's goodness in
the most unexpected of places: a prison, a hospital, a homeless shelter.
Even in the midst of madness—there is a still small voice of sanity
trying to be heard. As chaplains, your voices in the prison were small,
nearly drowned out by the madness. But some of us heard it—and
because we heard it, things are different.*

*I have learned to give thanks for those moment-to-moment bless-
ings that I feel I do not deserve. You chaplains taught me that it is the
mercy—and only the mercy—that is important. We deserve the worst—
but thanks to mercy, we get the best. The road to goodness, to holiness,
is the road of mercy.*

The Volunteer Army

Thankfully, the inmates didn't have to depend only on
chaplains for spiritual connection. We had a host of volunteers, and there's no way even our modest religious program, with so many varied groups, could have operated
without them. I marveled at the courage it took for them
to journey into the unknowns of prison life. Most were
more charismatic, or traditional, than I. My language was
not salted with as much "Jesus" or peppered with praise
songs in the same way. But they had a great heart for forgotten and disregarded people, and they were there on a regular
basis, accepting the daunting task of ongoing ministry rather
than the occasional drop-in.

I found myself seeing things in a different light, noting their compassion, their good will, their intent to offer healing and hope. And often they were better than I was in communicating with inmates. It was my own jailhouse conversion—to be less judgmental about their way of experiencing and sharing God's goodness, and to check my own shabby, self-righteous self at the door.

7

One Sacred Universe

We all require and want respect,
man or woman, black or white.
It's our basic human right.

—Aretha Franklin

It was a long road for me to see how my attitude toward others, open-minded as I thought I was, had been laced with disrespect or condescension, particularly toward the religiously conservative. But I also had a visceral reaction to the use of scripture to denigrate or manipulate others, and women were often the target of that kind of religious abuse. I wanted to sing Aretha Franklin's anthem on respect to inmates and staff alike, especially the line, "find out what it means to me." I understood why fundamentalist Christians veered toward keeping women in their place. They believed they were being biblically faithful, but it was also a convenient way to hang on to power and ignore the revelatory teachings of Jesus. A visit from a pair of Jewish seminarians reminded me that the impulse to keep women confined to their place crossed into other religious communities as well.

Izzy

Two Sephardic Jews were traveling to prisons in North and South Carolina, visiting Jewish inmates. Herschel was from New Hampshire; Ari, from New Zealand. Both were entering a rabbinical school in New Jersey in the fall. Wispy hairs on their faces attested to their young age.

Our only Jew at the time was an African American named Isaiah (or Izzy), who was a recent convert. He was so recently a convert that he didn't know much about his new faith except that he could get a kosher meal. Izzy had been in prison for twenty-three years. He changed religions frequently. Even so, I liked to think that he could be encouraged to be steadfast on his latest path, so I was very glad to welcome the rabbinical students for a personal visit.

I offered them a corner of the chapel to meet with Izzy. They told me that they couldn't meet in a room where Christian services were held. I offered to remove the cross, which I do often during other services, but that wasn't enough. The only other choice was my office with me present, to which they reluctantly agreed. They turned the chairs around so their backs were to me and began their prayers.

They strapped the long black leather phylacteries on Izzy's left arm and one on his head. They began to recite the *Shema* in Hebrew (*Hear, O Israel: the Lord our God, the Lord is one . . .*). Izzy repeated the Hebrew words after them as best he could.

Explain Moses

After a discussion of faith and practices, and more beautiful prayers, I offered to give Herschel and Ari a tour. They said they would like that since they hadn't toured any of the other prisons. Off we went to the medical clinic, the classrooms, the sewing plant. Down the hallway the inmates were on their way to the chow hall. My two visitors looked stricken to be passing so many men at one time. It is a bit overwhelming the first time to see a throng of inmates. I pulled them to the side and said, "Don't worry. You're safe with me." They didn't look so sure.

I took them to solitary confinement. "Are these men violent?" Ari asked.

"Some of them, sometimes."

"Are there assaults?" Herschel wanted to know.

"Sometimes."

"Are you afraid?"

"Sometimes."

I turned to Officer Wilcox and asked, "Officer, are you afraid?"

"No, never. I know that if anything happens, I can have back-up in thirty seconds. If I can hold a guy off for thirty seconds, I'll have plenty of officers here to help me."

Ari's eyes traveled down the long row of locked doors. "Why are these men in solitary?"

"All kinds of reasons," said Officer Wilcox. "One man is in here because a couple of weeks ago during his family visit, they were caught passing cocaine. And then there's the guy with the cellphone. We 'dry-celled' him to find it. That's when we stop the water in his cell so when he passes something in the toilet, we can find it. Amazing what they stick up their butts."

We walked through the housing units, through the hallways, out to the yard. "Is it like what you thought it would be?" I asked. Yes, they said, like pictures they'd seen before. "Prisons do have a way of all looking the same, don't they?" I said.

They asked about the types of assaults, if there were any suicides, and how drugs get in. Eventually we were back in the lobby. As they were leaving, Herschel asked, "Do most of them have a life sentence?"

"No, not most, but quite a few. You know that some of these men killed a person during a night on drugs or when they were enraged about something. They will pay for it the rest of their lives. Some of them committed crimes like that when they were younger than you. And some of them are trying to turn themselves around. They're careful to have no infractions, and they're doing all that they can to find a meaningful life, even in prison."

Herschel said, "But they took a life, and shouldn't they pay for that?"

"It's a good question to ask," I said. "Makes us wonder how to explain Moses, who also took a life, doesn't it?"*

Herschel looked at me dumbstruck. He said simply, "Thank you for your time."

You Have to Be Carefully Taught

Muslims in that part of North Carolina are few and, especially after 9/11, have been considered suspect. One workshop, led by a visiting Muslim chaplain, was a great help since the men didn't have a teacher on a regular basis. That was clear when two inmates came in asking for a video by Iman Aya-

---

* Exodus 2:11–15.

tollah Khomeini, the Iranian revolutionary leader. They didn't know who he was, they just thought he was a great leader, the "Grand Ayatollah." I'd been visited by federal agents once before when I inadvertently ordered Qurans from New Jersey that actually came from Iran. I wasn't going to make that mistake again.

The Muslim chaplain that day encouraged leadership, serving God with compassion, and importantly, setting straight the ways that Islam has been distorted. It was inspiring, and the men soaked it in. Toward the end of the workshop, I stepped into the hallway where an officer stood guard. He leaned over and said, "Is that suicide-bomber class over yet?"

I explained as evenly as I could that far from preaching violence, they were teaching the central practices of the faith: mercy and forgiveness.

"Oh," he said, and that was that.

Other officers were not like that. One time after Eid al-Fitr, the feast at the end of Ramadan, a lieutenant made a point of saying to me, "Chap, I know this is an important night for these Muslim inmates, and me and my officers will do all we can to respect their evening. If anything comes up, we'll do all we can not to be disruptive. But I have to tell you that when they leave, we'll have to pat them down for any smuggled food. I just want you to know because I didn't want you to think we're trying to give them a hard time."

Doing his job, with respect. Who could ask for more?

Disrespect on the Yard

The prayers of the Native Americans had a peacefulness to them—in part for their simplicity and grace, but perhaps, too, because they were offered outside. While all the others were locked in their cells for the midday count, the Native Americans gathered outside for their sacred pipe ceremony. In the side yard were huge grey boulders in a circle with an opening toward the east. Even the razor-wire fences couldn't block the hillside evergreens, the silent sentinels in a world beyond reach. For a moment, you could forget where you were.

In summer the heat rose in filmy waves from the rocks, sweat pouring down the faces of the men. In winter the Appalachian mountain winds blew so cold that their hands could barely bend around the pipe. Thin cotton uniforms proved a flimsy barrier between skin and the elements. Nevertheless, the faithful attended without complaint. Only a downpour of rain or below-freezing temperatures sent the ceremony indoors.

Each man entered the circle and was smudged and cleansed with the smoke drawn from a conch shell with burning sweetgrass, sage, and cedar. A boombox played the lulling sound of a wooden flute as the pipe-bearer prepared the sacred pipe with tobacco. His hands stretched wide like an orchestral conductor, holding the pipe in midair, poised to offer the ancient prayers.

Silence descended as each man followed the pattern— raising the pipe toward the sky to honor the Great Spirit, pointing it to the ground to honor Mother Earth. A few draws from the stem released smoke into the air before it was passed to the next man. After the pipe made its way around the circle, it was wrapped and tucked into a small wooden box. Then hand-over-hand by turn the men held the prayer feather close to their hearts as they voiced their common hopes—for their children or an ailing parent, for strength to face the challenges of the day, for healing of the earth, for healing of their own wounds and those they'd hurt. In a place of turmoil, on one tiny patch of land, in one little slip of time, peace prevailed.

But the peace didn't last. Word got around that the prayer circle was desecrated. Someone took the heel of their boot and shoved the gravel into the shape of a large cross. The men were incensed, and I didn't blame them.

They filed grievance forms. I went to the administration. But over the next few weeks, the vandalism was repeated several times. It was disturbing that the culprit had to be a staff member since only accompanied inmates could walk in that part of the yard.

Cease-and-desist warnings were issued, but no accusations were made. "This is not okay," one memo to staff read. "We are looking at who made rounds on the yards. Corrective action will be taken as necessary. Please heighten sensitivity to this situation."

The guys decided I was pretty worthless. "If a desecration like this happened to the Christians," they complained, "something would be done immediately." I couldn't figure out why I wasn't getting results either. With cameras everywhere, why wasn't someone caught in the act?

Two weeks passed before we were assured that the disturbance from a "misguided officer" would never happen again, with daily yard checks to confirm it remained undefiled. The pipe-bearer smudged the reconsecrated ground. I wanted to smudge out my preoccupation with who did it.

I considered the universe I'd landed in as I read Richard Rohr: "There are not sacred and profane things, places and moments. There are only sacred and desecrated things, places and moments—and it is we alone who desecrate them by our own blindness and lack of reverence. It is one sacred universe, and we are all a part of it."

Gregory

Thirty men came through the door with their prayer rugs draped across their shoulders, their kufis covering their

radation. By the time he was ten years old, he was recruited as a boy soldier in an unnamed army against neighborhood forces of drugs and poverty. He learned to wield his rage as both weapon and shield. The true source of his anger might be known only to him, but whatever it was, it didn't give him license to perpetuate the wounding. It took little to set off violence in the tinderbox of prison, and I was responsible for any potentially incendiary things that happened during services. Though it was not the time for one of my high-minded sermons, it was important for me to draw the line on abuse. His steely stare communicated his mind-set clearly, so I simply said, "Gregory, if you have problems with me I'd appreciate it if you'd come talk to me about them." Looking at the wall, he said, "Are you finished?"

I was, and he left as quickly as he'd walked in. I was left humbled, keenly aware of my limitations. I couldn't save him, but I could seek to minimize his damage, and pray that healing would find him someday. I hoped my call signaled somewhere in him that I wouldn't break, nor would I abandon. I was still his chaplain.

Andre

Andre was like Gregory, consumed with the need to hate something or someone. After fifteen years in prison, he too discovered Islam. But Andre paid attention to the Muslim volunteer leaders and chaplains. Through them he saw the faith exemplified in strength, compassion, and humility—and he wanted to be like them. He studied the Quran and the teachings of the Prophet. Five times a day he knelt to pray in his cell amid the endless noise of metal clanging doors and a bedlam of voices. He became a prayer leader and was given the opportunity to teach during the Jummah prayers.

After a difficult week of racially charged fights in the yard, Andre offered these words of encouragement: "Brothers, every day in our prayers we join hundreds of millions of people around the world praying with us. Five times a day we join our ancestors who've recited these prayers for fourteen hundred years. Five times a day we lower our bodies to the ground to submit to Allah, to praise Allah, to ask for guidance and forgiveness from Allah . . .

"If you hate the Europeans, then how are you different? It's not about what color you are. Don't let hate rule you, man. Don't let it take hold in your heart. Racism has no place in Islam. I've been hurt by many of my own race, yet some have the nerve to say that they can't trust 'Europeans' when we can't even trust our own.

"Every single man should be judged based on his character. You made choices that got you here. If you love dope or women more than Allah, then that's on you. Don't hate any people, because it brings nothing but hate. Understand your history. Become a man of knowledge. Some foul stuff's been done to us, and we've done some foul stuff ourselves. But it's no time for hating. Look in the mirror. Hate what you've done to yourself. We talk a good game, but it's time to live a good game."

Andre was moved to the lower security prison where by all accounts he continued to live and teach the good game.

8

The Angel of Death

Behold the gates of mercy
In arbitrary space
And none of us deserving
The cruelty or the grace.

—"Come Healing" by Leonard Cohen

"You're the angel of death, ain't ya?" Obby said bluntly but not unkindly. I hadn't thought of myself that way, but he was right. I was usually the one who told inmates about a death in the family. So when Obby was summoned to my office, he knew the news wasn't good. I invited him to sit down, but he preferred to stand, leaning on his wooden cane with both hands.

"So my brother died, didn't he?" he asked.

"Yes. How'd you know?"

"He's been sick. A cousin wrote and told me. He's about the only kin I had left. I'm seventy-seven years old, young lady. You'll find out when you get my age, everybody dies."

"Anyone in your family you want to talk to, Obby?"

"No, not really." I invited him to sit for a minute, but he said he thought he'd move on. I asked him how long he'd been in prison.

"About thirty years," he said. "Guess I'll die here."

"What did you do before you came here?"

"I started my own graveyard."

"Really? You were the owner of a cemetery?"

"No, honey. I said I started my own graveyard." Obby had a rather charming if succinct way about him. "There're some huntin' accidents that ain't no accidents. I was hired. I got caught. Here I am. That's that."

He lifted his cane with "that's that" and then swayed from side-to-side as he slowly went out the door.

As the bearer of bad news, I understood why some of the inmates thought of me with trepidation. But I found the death notices to be a sacred time. Brittle exteriors could crack open with tenderness. Smothered regrets could be released in exhaled confessions. For their safety and sanity, inmates often exuded steely-eyed containment—keep it together, show no weakness, that sort of thing. But it wasn't real, not the way they really felt. The chapel was about the only safe place to show emotion, and my office frequently became a sanctuary for it.

One inmate was so worried about his dad that he started crying as soon as he came to see me, hardly able to get the phone number out for a call. As soon as they started talking, they both started sobbing, the inmate telling his dad how much he loved him, how he knew he could beat that cancer. His dad died two weeks later. Most inmates, however, didn't get that last goodbye.

Dion

A sheriff's office called with the news of a mother's suicide. I dreaded telling Dion. He last spoke with his mother only months before, during her hospital stay for a bashed face and broken bones at the hands of her boyfriend. As her only child, Dion spoke tenderly to her then as he had many times before. "I'm glad you're safe now, mom. You're gonna be ok. I love you, mom."

Dion arrived at my office, but before I could say a word, he said, "It's my mom, right?"

I told him the little I knew, that she died of an overdose, that they were calling it a suicide.

"I knew this day would come," he said with a sigh, "but I still can't believe it. She had problems. I loved her. She was my only link to the outside. Now I have no one."

His voice locked in his throat, and he swallowed hard. "There's no one to call. It was just the two of us. We went through a lot together. I think I did more raising her than she did me. I did love her."

I wanted to offer something to this grieving veteran of home front wars. "Dion, you want some coffee?" He nodded. Sipping this small measure of comfort, he told me how grateful he was for kindnesses given by staff and other inmates. He told me about the night the captain woke him up at three in the morning. His mother called the prison because she wanted to tell him good-bye before she killed herself. "The captain told me to keep talking to her," he explained, "until he traced the call somewhere in Louisville.

"I assured her of my love, told her to hang in there and that everything was going to be all right. Thanks to the captain, the police got to her in time and took her to a hospital. She was saved that time. I guess there was no good-bye call last night."

He paused for a last swig of coffee. "Guess we've been saying good-bye our whole lives."

The coroner called three weeks later to say no one picked up Dion's mother's body. When I told him about the cremation, Dion simply said, "Thanks for letting me know. It's a last good-bye."

Favorite Uncle

"Please be careful when you tell Desmond that his favorite uncle died," his mother said to me. "He'll be real upset when you tell him, so be prepared. He's got problems when he gets upset. He doesn't know how to handle things. Tell him I'll see him during visitation this weekend and tell him all about the service."

Desmond came into my office out of breath from being out on the yard. He was already shaking.

"It's bad news, ain't it?"

"I'm afraid it is. Sit down, Desmond. Your mother called. She wants you to know that your favorite uncle died."

"Oh, no! Not my favorite uncle!" he cried.

"Yes, your Uncle Jimmy died yesterday."

"Uncle Jimmy?" He paused. "But I don't got a Uncle Jimmy."

"You don't?" I was confused. So I called his mother back.

"Uncle Jimmy wasn't his favorite uncle?" she said. "I thought he was. Well, don't that beat all?"

Grave Robbing

We did have a few miracles along the way. I got Jason's mother on the phone one day and asked her how she was doing, considering we'd heard she'd died.

"Oh, I'm a little tired, but maybe not dead tired," she chuckled. "But according to Jason, I've died three or four times. I wish Jason wouldn't do that. He's a pathological liar, and we don't know why. He was the sweetest boy you could ever imagine."

I told Jason about his mother's good health. He wanted to know if she was mad about it. "More sad than mad," I reported. "Why do you keep lying like that?"

"I thought it would get me some sympathy," he explained. "I got a guy on my block trying to come at me with sexual advances. I'm not into that kind of thing, Chap. I got my standards."

Calvin was "so torn up" about the death of his grand-mother—said she'd been hit by a school bus—he asked to be placed in seg so he could grieve in private. A lieutenant brought him to my office instead. After connecting with his family, I told him, "Great news, Calvin. Your grandmother isn't dead after all. It's a miracle, isn't it?"

The lieutenant asked him what was going on. "I don't appreciate you wasting Chap's time or my time. And God doesn't like your lying lips either."

Calvin confessed that he'd fought with his fiancé and needed to talk to her again, but he was out of phone calls. So that's when he came up with the throwing-grandma-under-the-bus scheme. He cried and begged for leniency. "Please don't write me up. I promise I won't do it again."

"No, you won't do it again, Mr. Anderson," said the lieu-tenant. "There's only so many resurrections Chap can manage, you know."

When the Fog Rolls In

When I walked in the prison one morning, I knew that some-thing was up. You can feel doom in your bones there. It's like getting an ache in your joints when the weather turns. The despair never leaves, but sometimes the fog rolls in and the ache gets severe. No one can see straight either.

I asked an officer why everyone seemed so somber. "What, you haven't heard? Inmate committed suicide last night in seg. Hung himself with a sheet."

I knew the man—midway through his time as a habitual felon, robbing and stealing to support a lifelong drug habit. His mother had visited him the week before. It was a noncontact visit, but even through the glass window she knew that he was depressed.

"He was really down," she said through tears when I called her. "I told him I was worried. He promised me he'd talk to a psychologist. I couldn't help him. I'm his mother, and I couldn't help him. He thought for sure he could get out, live close to me, and work in heating and air. He thought he'd finally get his life together, and we'd be together. Now it will never happen. I'm his mother, and I couldn't help him . . .oh, God . . .oh, God . . . oh, God."

Big John

When an officer told Big John to report to my office early one morning, he wasn't alarmed—I often called him to my office to talk about the Native American circle where he'd served as a committed prayer leader. He sat down in his usual easy manner.

I never found a good way to convey a death, even an expected one. Telling it straight out seemed the kindest way. "I have sad news for you, Big John," I said as steadily as possible. "Your mother passed away this morning."

He nodded. He sat straight in his chair with his hands resting gently on his legs. His eyes fixed on the green ivy cascading over my file cabinet. He sat in silence, curling his lower lip. His mother came to visit every week for ten years. After her heart attack, she had to be pushed in a wheelchair by her granddaughter, but still she came. As her health continued to fail, Big John knew what was coming. He told me some months before that he'd been growing his hair for years, knowing that when his mother died, he'd cut it. "I'll take a hawk feather and bead it into my hair," he'd said. "When I visit her coffin, I'll place it there as a part of me that goes with her."

We sat in silence as the morning light shimmered on his long black ponytail. He finally said, "I'd like to talk to my family now."

He spoke with daughters, sister, brother, aunts and uncles, nieces and nephews. He told them he was happy that he'd seen his mother during the Saturday visit. Her parting words were, "I'm doing fine, son. Don't worry about me." She died in her sleep two days later.

When the ten-minute allotment of phone time was over, he asked me to call his friend Eagle. They'd known each other for years in one prison or another, both of them with long sentences. Tall and soaring in height, Eagle fit his name. As he stepped into the office, I said, "Eagle, John just received some very sad news."

"It's your mom, isn't it? Sorry, man." Big John stood to receive Eagle's embrace.

Then the planned ritual began. Big John said, "Chap, it's time for the scissors." I unlocked my desk drawer and placed the scissors in Eagle's hands. Big John turned around. The long shiny black hair was clipped at the neck. Eagle handed back the scissors. Big John took his ponytail and held it tight. They sat down. Five, ten, fifteen minutes passed in silence.

Big John stood. Then Eagle and I stood with him.

"I'll wait to see her again." Then he reached out a

hand to shake mine. "Thank you, Chap. Thank you." They turned to leave together, Eagle's hand resting on Big John's shoulder.

A Bit of Life, and Hope

It was late spring. Well-tended flowers bloomed beside the walkway to the gatehouse. Singing birds clung to the razor-wire fence. I swung open the buzzing door, greeted the officers, swiped my ID card, handed over my book bag for inspection, and walked through the metal detector without the alarm sounding. I was grateful for that one silent reprieve.

Stepping again onto the pavement, I walked through a narrow bed of pink and white flowers under a bright blue sky before entering the relentless world of grey. I waved to a green-uniformed inmate on a riding mower as he made loops through the new grass. I'd known Roger from the minimum-custody unit where he trained Bixby, one of the stars of the dog-training program. Roger stopped the mower, jumped down, and scooped up a handful of grass clippings. Slowly he walked toward me with his hands holding out the offering.

"Chap, can you help me?" A baby bird was squawking on the grassy cushion in his hands. "This bird keeps hopping out of the bushes right in front of the mower. I'm afraid it'll get hurt. Can you save it?"

"Okay, let's try putting the bird deep into those bushes, and I'll keep watch."

With the bird carefully cupped in his hands, he crawled under the bush and set it down. Shimmying out, he plopped back onto the mower. I quickly squatted down as the mower started up its roar.

"Stop! Go back!" I shouted toward the bush, fanning my fingers in front of the wee thing. "It's dangerous out here!

Shoosh!" It didn't listen. I watched helplessly as the bird hopped out of the cool darkness into the sunlight. The mower moved past just in time. With the bird's wings flapping and our arms waving, Roger and I whooped and hollered, allies in saving a tiny life.

"Thanks, Chap," he called after me.

"Thank you for noticing that little fella," I said. As I walked inside, the words of poet Emily Dickinson came to mind: *Hope is the thing with feathers.*

Jamal and Kejuan

Jamal and Kejuan talked in jumbles over one another, jabbing each other like bear cubs. "Slow down, guys. I've got whatever time you need," I assured them.

They were twenty-two years old and grew up in the same household. "We're brothers even though we're really cousins," explained Jamal. "Listen, Chap, Kejuan is walking into trouble and you gotta help. He's getting out of prison in two weeks."

"Yeah," Kejuan jumped in, "and the case manager told me I gotta go back to the county I came from. Same town. It's trouble. Big trouble."

I asked the obvious question, "You explained this to the case manager, right?"

"Yeah, but he said there's nothing he can do. Said his hands were tied. I can't go back there. It'll be bad, real bad."

Jamal pleaded, "Chap, you gotta do something. You're our last hope."

I told them if I was their last hope, they were in big trouble. I told them I would call the case manager and look into transitional programs in their county. "Are there any other options you can think of? Is there a relative in another part of the state you could stay with?"

Kejuan jumped to his feet and shouted, "There's nobody. Can't somebody help me? I got my GED. I got plans for my life. But I'm a dead man walking. Can't somebody believe me?"

I was unnerved by his plea. "I believe you, but I'm just not sure how to help you."

Jamal stood and gently swung an arm into Kejuan's side. "Come on, bro. She can't help us."

I called his case manager. He'd done what he could within the limits of parole stipulations. Parolees were required to return to the county where their crime was committed.

I called my supervisor but was told there was nothing to be done. We were surrounded and outnumbered by an unseen army of policies and procedures.

Ten days after Kejuan was released from prison, Jamal sat stone-silent in my office. I started to tell him the news, but the words got stuck. Jamal knew. With eyes blinking and chin steeled, he mounted an effort not to cry. I did too.

"It's Kejuan," I said, barely audible.

His hands covered his face as he cried out, "God, no! God, no!"

"Kejuan was shot and killed last night. I'm so sorry." My words were hardly a whisper, but they were heard like a blast. His body shook and groaned.

"We told you he was walking into trouble," he cried. "Now see what happened? He's dead. He shouldn't be dead. He was getting his life together. This shouldn't have happened. He was only twenty-two. We told you. We told you."

He left me in that three-word echo chamber, one I can still hear today.

9

Family Matters

The way we are, we are members of each other.
All of us. Everything.
The difference ain't in who is a member and who
is not, but in who knows it and who don't.

—Burley Coulter, in *The Wild Birds* by Wendell Berry

Leon

Leon remembered when he was six years old, running to his dad's closet to see if his clothes were still hanging there. He was sure his mother was wrong when she said his dad wasn't coming home. "But he wouldn't leave his clothes," Leon reasoned. After school each day, he sat in the closet comforted by the shirts and pants draped around him. "It smelled like dad. I knew he'd come back, until the day I opened the closet door, and it was empty. So that was it for me. I decided I didn't need anybody. If my dad didn't care, I didn't care."

Listening to Leon through the rutted paths of "didn't care," I knew the litany of woes to follow. Dropped out of school.

Joined a gang. Sold drugs. Robbed. Assaulted. Convicted. His passage to prison was a familiar entry in the records—AWD-WWITKISI, assault with a deadly weapon with intent to kill or inflict serious injury. Patterns were the same, just names and locations changed.

The week before he had told me about a letter from his aunt with news of a big surprise—she was bringing his dad for a visit. He didn't know what to do, what to think. "I haven't seen my dad since I was a little kid. Thought I didn't care. But when I became a Christian, I decided the right thing to do was to care. So I started caring about my dad and praying for him because that's what Jesus would want me to do. I decided I wanted my dad to be proud of me—that maybe I'd get to meet him one day and show him how I'd turned my life around. The day's here, and now I don't know how to act."

A few days later I got the report from Leon. He bounced in the chair like a little boy in his smartly dressed newest uniform, an indulgence I knew cost him a few coffees slipped to the inmate in charge of their clothes. He told me that he'd stayed up all night long imagining how to begin the conversation with his dad. He went to the visitation room still not knowing what to say or expect.

"I stood beside a table," he reported, "and in walked my aunt and my daddy. I went right for my aunt and gave her a big hug and kiss. Then I stood in front of my daddy, still not sure what to say or do. But before I could figure it out, my daddy threw his arms around me and started crying. I'm not talking about just any little tears. I'm talking about sobs, loud enough for everyone in visitation to hear.

"People started turning around, staring at us. I was embarrassed. I tried to quiet him down, 'Dad, Dad, it's okay.' But it didn't work. He just kept on sobbing. And while his arms were still around me, he said, 'Son, I've been waiting to hug you for years. I'm sorry, son. I'm sorry. Can you forgive me? I love you, son.' When my daddy said those words, I started crying right along with him. I didn't want him to let go. And you know what? I didn't care if anybody was looking."

Leon started crying again. "It was a miracle, Chap. I got myself a real miracle."

Antwan

I brought my little stool and parked it outside the trap window at the bottom of a seg cell. Kneeling was too hard on my knees, so I sat like a kid in kindergarten, knees up around my head. I started talking to the back of a bald head. Antwan sat on the concrete floor, hands gripped together, head down.

"What's going on, Antwan? I heard you want a phone call to your mother, but you know I can't give you one unless it's an emergency. So what's happening? You worried about her diabetes?"

"I figured you wouldn't give me a call, Chap. I'm just tired. I wanna hear my mama's voice, ya know? Thirteen years of this and no end to it. I been thinkin' 'bout my case. When I lost my appeal, I was death-struck. Death was all over me, even an evangelist told me death was on me. The jury gave me life," he sighed. "This is no life. I've wished a thousand times over that I could've been given the death penalty. I've prayed, but my life is cursed. There's really no need to pray. God let me down. I never asked God for anything until my trial. God let me down. I told my mom to please honor my feelings and don't ask me to carry things to God. My mom says that I'm being tested. I've been tested for all these years, and there's nothing, nothing for me. Nothing has changed."

"Antwan, you still love your mama, don't you?" I said. "Then write to her and tell her. Tell her you think about her every day. Tell her you hope she's taking good care of herself. Tell her you hope she gets to feeling better. Tell her you're sorry you're not there to help her. You don't have to mention God. Just write and say 'I love you, Mama.' Okay?"

All I could see was the bald head nodding. Inmates may not have given much thought to their mamas outside of prison, but inside, they needed them, and needed to be with them. When I told one inmate that his mother was in ICU with heart failure, he kept shaking his head and saying, "I messed up, Chap. She needs me, and I messed up." With a sentence of life plus 142 years, taking care of his mama was one thing he was never going to do.

I got calls from mothers desperately needing to know their sons were all right. One was worried because winter had come to the mountains, and her son wrote to say it was cold in his cell. She wanted to send him blankets but that wasn't allowed. "I can't say the word 'prison,'" she added, trying to hold back tears. "My son was such a good boy, so smart, so sweet. It was the wrong crowd and the drugs. They change people."

Early one morning I picked up the phone and heard what sounded like an elderly woman. She spoke carefully and respectfully, explaining that her son was HIV-positive and that the last time they spoke, over two weeks before, he said he wasn't feeling well. "I'm worried that my son will die and no one will tell me."

I assured her that she didn't need to worry, that someone from the prison would let her know."

"Really? Do you think that's true?"

"Yes, ma'am. I know it's true."

"God bless you, Chaplain. God bless you."

I hung up the phone, assuming there were at least a few things a mother could count on.

My Eyes Are My Own

An inmate with a life sentence wrote, "I know people wonder why I don't make eye contact with them. Some people think it's fear. Others think it's because I'm weird or crazy. The real reason is that I remember my mother's eyes the day I took the stand to testify against her. I was ten years old. I remember my father's eyes when I sat there and said not a word of the carefully prepared speech he had instructed me to say the night before. I remember my brother's eyes as he watched me cry.

"My eyes are my own, but it is so easy to forget how much I say with them. So I see without watching, watch without staring, and pray that the few glimpses I offer others into the windows that are my eyes reveal a landscape better than the ones I have known."

What Messes You Up

An inmate with a forty-year sentence wrote, "My mama was the outcast of her family. She shot, stabbed, or beat every man who crossed her. She was raped and abused as a child. She shot a gun aimlessly. We dodged her gunfire. I was ready to aid the 'mad fool' that was my mama. Nearly every problem in our family was solved with verbal or physical abuse. That was normal for us. I baked a cake for my mama when I was eleven years old. She slapped it to the floor. I always wanted to kill her. Then when I got older, I just wanted to kill myself. I can't remember what age it started, but sexual abuse came from mom. I learned what sex was from her. That messes you up. I'm in here for rape."

Dante

The medical staff appreciated·the pride that Dante took in his janitorial duties in their offices. He worked with a smile but with little talk, careful to stay out of the way as much as possible in the busy medical hub. If he finished his work early, he spent time at the weight-lifting pile out in the yard. His discipline kept his twenty-nine-year-old body trim and muscular. He was infraction free, determined to keep his actions in clear sight of his release date only a few years away.

One evening after chow, Dante had a searing pain in his chest. He was rushed to the hospital. Heart attack. He was placed in the intensive care unit. Officers were assigned to take shifts to stay with him, his wrists chained to the bed. Visiting him in ICU, I was shocked to see him so weak and barely able to speak.

With his eyes closed he whispered, "Chap, tell everyone in medical that I'll be back as soon as I can, and thank them for their prayers."

The doctors planned to move him to a prison hospital the next day for recovery. I shared the good news with the medical staff, but I failed to ask permission to tell Dante's mother. The hospitalization of inmates was generally not information passed along to family members. There were security risks, as one can imagine, if a family visited a prisoner's hospital room. Yet there were exceptions. If the inmate was in critical condition and not expected to live, the chaplain could receive approval from the superintendent to call the family. A special visit could be arranged.

But there was no call or visit approved for Dante. Why would there be? He would go back to the prison soon, we thought.

Dante died three days after his heart attack. We were all stunned. I agonized over my actions. I second-guessed my choices. I wished I'd asked permission to call his mother while I was with him in the hospital. I wished I'd asked approval to call and tell her about his condition. The superintendent made the dreaded call to his family to tell them of his death. Then I called his mother and offered my condolences.

"We all liked your son," I said, trying to sound comforting. "He was doing a great job. Everyone knew of his strong faith in God. I know you'll miss him terribly. We'll miss him too."

First there was silence on the other end of the line. Then sobbing. Then the aching words poured out. "But why didn't you call and tell me? Aren't you the chaplain? Why didn't anyone tell me that my son had a heart attack? Couldn't someone have at least told me that? My son is dead, and I didn't even get to hear his voice. This was my son, my only son, my baby. Doesn't anyone there have a heart? Wouldn't you have wanted to know if it'd been your son?"

"Yes, I would," I whispered. "It's not right. There's nothing right about it. I failed you. I'm terribly sorry." My voice cracked and I stopped. There weren't enough "I'm sorrys" to stretch across that canyon of sorrow.

"The Department of Corrections has nothing to say to me. Nothing. And you say you're a chaplain? I hope you get a heart someday." With that, she hung up —and with that, I put my head on my desk and cried.

Joel

Joel pleaded with me to grant a phone call to his mother. "She's sick, I swear. Give me a Bible. I'll swear on it. I gotta talk to her. I'm a wreck. Look at me. My hands are shakin'. Can't sleep. Haven't talked to her in a month."

With no proof of sickness, I denied the phone call and recommended letter writing.

"You know you used to be a nice lady when you first came here, but not anymore. Somethin' happened to you. Now you're like all the rest. Just here for a paycheck."

I covered my mouth and looked down at my papers, hiding the fact that "just here for a paycheck" was one of the funniest things I'd heard in a long time. I knew Joel from his previous incarcerations. He would swear that he'd never do drugs again, and I believed him every time.

Joel took another swing. "There are some guys out on the yard who say you're lookin' old 'cause somebody put a curse on you."

"I'm looking old, Joel, because I am old. How old are you?"

He stared down at his hands, weaving his fingers back and forth. "I'm forty-three years old and I'm sittin' here thinkin' that my mama oughta send me money. What's a grown man like me doin' waitin' on his mama to send him money?"

He walked away without another word.

Devon

"I just found out that I'm a daddy," Devon announced. Some of the guys talked about their kids, but Devon, who I saw often, hadn't mentioned any, not even a girlfriend. "I have a twelve-year-old daughter," he explained. "Her mother, who was my girlfriend for a little while, sent me these pictures."

"You didn't know?"

"I didn't know. She was my girlfriend for only about a month. We just had sex one time. She just told my daughter who her daddy is."

Devon received the news about his daughter on the same day he found out that he lost the appeal on his case. He faced a life sentence.

"Here's the one where she's taking her first step," he said, showing me the baby pictures. Then it was the school pictures. He held each one as if he'd discovered the Dead Sea Scrolls. Holy pictures.

Then he showed me the photo that had been taken of him that morning. He had no money coming in so another inmate paid for the picture. And the water on his cell block had been cut off. "I got a trickle of water out of the faucet and shaved my face. I got a clean T-shirt too. What do you think?" he asked.

"Wonderful—a great picture of you," I said. "Your daughter looks just like you, the dark hair, the dark eyes, the smile. She's going to love this picture."

"Chap, I want to have a special visit with her. I want to do this right. I don't want to mess it up. I want to be a real daddy to her, encourage her, help her out. We have a lot to catch up on."

Then he added, "Do you mind if I get twelve birthday cards? I want to send her a card for every year of her life that I've missed."

"Of course, Devon. She'll love it."

Norman

Norman showed me a letter from home. He was a small man with deep brown eyes, shoulder-length brown hair tucked behind his ears and a straggly beard. His crisscrossed front teeth were exposed when he spoke. He held out a small newspaper clipping. "That's my son. He's eleven. See, he's in a hospital bed. That snow globe in his hands was given to him by a nurse 'cause he missed the first snowfall. Can you find out how he's doing?"

I called the hospital, but the boy had been released. I called his home, but there was no answer.

I asked him when was the last time he saw his son.

"Oh, it's been 'bout six years, all the time I been in prison. I don't want my kids comin' to a place like this to see me."

"How much time do you have left?" I asked.

"About twenty years."

"Murder?"

"Yeah. I took the law into my own hands. I killed the guy who molested my daughter. She was eight years old. The man who done it was my ex-wife's boyfriend."

"Why didn't you just let the courts take care of it?"

"Because I knew he wouldn't get much time for a first offense. I couldn't let him do what he did to my daughter to anybody else. I done what anybody would do to protect their kids."

I asked if he felt any regret about it.

"No, I hate it, but I don't regret it. I hate that I killed him in front of his mother. I shoulda waited 'til he was alone. It wasn't good for her, you know. And I hate it that I didn't do somethin' with the body. Maybe I coulda hid it. But you know what I did after I shot him? I went down to the police station with the gun and turned myself in. I didn't run. I didn't hide. I know it was wrong what I done, but all I could picture when I done it was my daughter in the hospital. If you coulda seen my girl, my baby girl, in that hospital bed. She was screechin' up on me. She wouldn't even let me hug her. I knew why."

"Was it out of rage that you pulled the trigger?"

"Nah, I was calm. I knew what I had to do. I was calm when I pulled the trigger. I was calm when I turned myself in. I was trained to be calm in a situation like that. Trained by the military, you know. We were trained to do the killing we had to do, and just keep on goin'. If someone needs killin', you just gotta do it and go on. I'm glad they found Saddam. I hope they get Bin Laden. I got my Bin Laden. The world's a better place."

"But, Norman, now your kids are without you."

"Yeah, but I took care of 'em financially. They're secure. They're old enough now to understand why I had to do what I did. And I hope when I die my name's in the Book of Life, and all I done is chalked up to lessons learned. Maybe God'll look with favor on me. I righted a wrong. Don't the Bible say 'an eye for an eye'?"

"Yes, then Jesus said, 'but I say to you, love your enemies.'"

"I think that's too hard."

Thinking it might be a teachable moment, I said, "Loving your enemies doesn't mean condoning their actions. It means you don't become like them. It means you stop the cycle of vengeance. There are other ways to stop abusers."

"Okay, then, so maybe I just shoulda broken his back."

With those words, Norman tucked the newspaper clipping in the letter and walked to the door.

"You'll call me if you hear about my son, won't ya?"

"Of course I will."

Wives and Other Strangers

I was glad when Chap Bill took the call from a woman needing a "congugial visit" with her inmate husband. "You mean a 'conjugal' visit?" he clarified.

Bill said she was near breathless saying she needed to have sex with her husband, that it was urgent, and did we set up that kind of visit?

Urgent or otherwise, she was fresh out of luck—none of those "visits" were allowed in North Carolina prisons. Bill told her he'd be glad to pass on the information to her husband that she loved him and missed him.

Not surprisingly, a lot of marriages don't survive incarceration. An inmate told me that after eleven years, his wife was asking for a divorce. As he waved a sheaf of papers in my face, he screamed that he wanted to hit her.

"Do her a favor," I said. "Sign those divorce papers. If you want to hit her, she doesn't need a man like you in her life."

Sensing a new mission field for those inmates who were dead set on getting married, Chap Bill and I got permission to offer premarital counseling. Terry and Trina were our first couple. Terry was at the halfway mark on his twenty-year sentence.

Trina, wearing a tight-fitting blouse and jeans and sitting as close to Terry as possible, kissed him a few times as they held hands throughout the session. She explained that they'd gone to the same high school but never dated. She ran into Terry's mom and found out about his incarceration for manslaughter. "I've been coming to see him for about four years now," she said, beaming at him.

"What do you like about him?" Bill asked.

"I like his laugh. And I like it that he is committed to Jesus and that we make all our decisions based on the Bible."

"Terry, what do you like about Trina?" I asked.

"I like her hair, her eyes, and her nu-nus."

"Her what?"

"You know, her nu-nus."

Trina giggled, turning her face to meet his grin.

"Terry, you're thirty years old," Bill said to him. "You can use grown-up language to speak about women."

"Okay. That's cool. Well, I like her boobs."

Darrell

Darrell wanted to call his wife, explaining that she'd just had a baby, but he wasn't the father. His wife had an affair with a man at her church, but he was long gone. Darrell promised his wife that he would raise the baby along with their two children as his own. After all, he told her, he had a few affairs, too. "I forgive her," he said, "but it still makes me mad."

I found out his wife and baby had been in the hospital for a few days because of complications—the baby was jaundiced, and she had high blood pressure. But when I reached her, she said she felt well enough to talk to her husband.

Darrell bellowed into the phone, "Why didn't you call me as soon as the baby was born? It's been four days! Does that baby look like him? When you going to get your butt over here to see me? When you going to send me money?"

I pushed the button down on the phone to end the conversation.

"Why'd you do that?" Darrell cried.

"Congratulations—you've just won the award for the Most Insensitive Inmate of the Month."

"How'd I do that?"

"Your wife just had a baby. You didn't ask her how she and the baby were doing or how she felt. Every question was about you. It was all about you. Why'd you do that?"

Darrell laced his tattooed fingers together and rocked them back and forth. He confessed that he didn't really know if he could raise the baby as his own, that he was really still mad at her.

"And how many times did you mess around?" I asked softly, contrary to my impulse to knock him up the side of his head. "And what about the mess that caused you to be here?"

Darrell seemed startled and went silent.

"You and your wife have hurt each other," I offered. "Whether you can make it through together, I don't know. But right now, I'm concerned about the new baby. This baby needs a loving father. You could be that father. You're getting out of prison this year. You've got to decide. It takes a strong man to put aside his feelings and do the right thing. Can you do that?"

He said, "I don't know."

"Darrell, telling your wife to get her 'butt' over here is extremely disrespectful. I hope that you never talk to your wife or any woman like that again."

"But it's just the way we talk to each other," he said defensively. Then he asked if he could have another call.

"Okay. But there are some things I want to hear you say. Apologize to her. Ask her how she's feeling. Ask about the baby. Tell her you'd love to see her and all the kids when she gets strong enough to make the trip to the prison. Tell her that you want to do the right thing and be a good dad to the kids. Tell her that you're sorry that you haven't been there for her. That'll do for starters."

Darrell did it. Then as he left my office, he even apologized to me.

Lloyd

Respectfulness was as foreign a notion to some as an expedition to the moon. A sense of possession of a girlfriend or wife was pervasive, often fueled by jealousy and entitlement. There were the charming, dangerous men, of course, or the clueless ones—or worst of all, the ones who were both. In prison less than a year, Lloyd seemed willfully obtuse about life behind bars. "I'm not like these guys," he explained. "I can cook gourmet meals. I fix antique cars. I garden. I dance. I read. I'm a Christian." Still acting like the friendly car salesman he used to be, he'd extend his hand for a shake with staff or inmates alike. That didn't go over well. With his wavy hair slicked back, his shirt carefully tucked and jacket buttoned, he was an easy target of derision.

One of his girlfriends sent the chaplains a dozen pages of pictures of Lloyd in his former life. There were photos of him dancing, harvesting his garden vegetables, polishing his car. Across the final page, she wrote in purple ink, "See, my Lloyd is innocent. He never could've done those terrible things to those girls."

Just before choir rehearsal, Lloyd asked if I would see him. His cadence was clipped with gasps. "Chap, you can't believe what happened this afternoon in the yard. I picked up a butterfly resting on a blade of grass. It was so beautiful. I held it in the palm of my hand. Then a guy came over and grabbed that butterfly and crushed it in his hands. I yelled at him, asking why he did it. All he could say was 'Get over it. You're in prison now.' Can you believe people can be so cruel?"

"Yes, sadly, I can, Lloyd." I could also believe that terrible things could happen to young girls in expertly polished cars.

Clearly, there was room for improvement for a lot of inmates and their families. But we always encouraged them to reach out to family, to try to work on their relationships, and to build healthier ones. We knew it was better for everyone to feel connected, to care about something, to feel cared for if that was possible.

The hope of seeing a mother, father, wife, or child again helped some inmates focus on keeping their heads down, no infractions, nothing that would keep them from an eventual reunion. For some it meant even more than that.

Jarvis

Not long before his release, Jarvis said to Chap Bill and me, "I'm going to live with my mother and help her out. She'll help me by giving me a place to live. I'm going to get a job. I'm going to stay away from drugs and all those people who push me off track. I'm not coming back here."

It all sounded great. Jarvis had been in several times for theft, the last one for stealing to support his addiction. But he loved his mother, and it seemed like the best shot he had for not having a return engagement with us.

A few months later, Chap Bill came in with a letter. There was a big glitch in Jarvis's plan. His mother died suddenly, and he couldn't keep her apartment. He lost his encouraging mother as well as a place to live. His fragile foothold on creating a stable life crumbled. Chaplain Bill answered his letter:

Dear Jarvis,

One of these days we will be like leaves that play in the wind. We will open ourselves to the sunlight, not afraid to allow the passing seasons to change our colors. We will fall from the tree as grace falls in the winter snow. We will fall so that the tree may live. Our lives are not just poems that are written about them. They are life itself, living poetry. Sometimes the wind catches hold of our souls and the vibrations produce beautiful sounds. The relationship you have with your mother is much like that sound. Don't think of her being gone, for she lives in your heart. To live in the hearts of those we leave behind is not to die. We are spirit. And her spirit lives not only in the heavens, but in your heart as well. Feelings are important, but spirit is much more than that . . . You already have everything you need right now. You are truly blessed.

I love you, my brother. Hang in there—

Chap

Jarvis returned to prison again after stealing from a convenience store. Maybe he wanted to believe he had everything he needed, as Chap Bill said, but somehow it wasn't true enough for him. I kept a copy of the letter, though. "You already have everything you need right now. You are truly blessed." Sometimes that was just what I needed to hear.

Not Forgetting the Other Families

I was surprised to see thirty people in the church fellowship hall on a cold winter night to hear my presentation on prison ministry. I was accustomed to speaking to small groups in my work of recruiting volunteers for our diverse religious programs. Thirty was a large number for the topic. I was warmly welcomed as I offered statistics, stories, and discussion. There were the usual questions about "jailhouse conversions." Yes, some people do change, I said. "What do you do with all the con artists?" The same thing I do with media, political, and commercial con artists; I try not to buy into their con games. "Are you afraid?" Sometimes, I answered. Then I shared ideas for how they could volunteer their time. They thanked me and sent me on my way with a prayer.

A petite woman with a kind face stopped me as I was leaving. With a similar amount of face wrinkles as mine, I guessed that we were about the same age.

She said softly, "A few years ago my eighty-year-old mother was robbed, beaten, and raped in her own home. As a result, she requires twenty four-hour care. The man who committed the assault is in your prison. I look at my sweet mother, who never hurt anyone, who is living a hell on earth, and I wonder, 'Where is God?' I can't possibly forgive that man for what he did to her."

I shivered with the horror of it. I wanted some word that could sound comforting in her devastation, but if there were such words, I did not know them.

FINDING A WAY OUT

10

Do Not Pass Me By

My very chains and I grew friends,
So much a long communion tends
To make us what we are . . .

—Lord Byron

The interrupting voice of the loudspeaker announced,
"Code One clear. Code One clear."* Easy for them to say, I
thought. Nothing was clear. Nothing.

In that haze it took me a minute to notice Lenny standing
in my doorway. As a library clerk, he often brought us religious
books that strayed to the wrong shelves.

"Hey, Lenny. You got some books for us?"

"No, ma'am. I got something to tell you."

His long straight hair was parted in the middle, flopping
over his face. Over and over, his hands raked back the ends just
enough to show a glimpse of his eyes.

---

* "Code one clear" means that the count of the inmates, taken several times
a day, has been accepted.

"Chap, I did something bad, real bad. I just swallowed some razor blades."

Immediately I phoned medical. They told me to give them a minute while they cleared an examining room.

"Why'd you do it, Lenny?"

"I don't know. I just felt real, real sad."

I fell into silence, swallowing the sharp edges of my own thoughts of inadequacies. I was a lousy chaplain and wasn't making a bit of difference, and didn't even know what to say to this man. My face must've contorted something awful because Lenny said, "Chap! Chap! You okay?"

"I'm okay," I lied. I didn't want to tell him how sick I felt that we failed him, that we hadn't figured out how to heal the mind enough to keep people from tearing up their insides.

"You know, Lenny," I finally said. "It's just that some days have more sadness than any of us can swallow. Promise me this—the next time you feel like putting a razor blade in your belly, how about coming to see a chaplain first? We know how to sit with all kinds of sadness. And we even have a few stories that might make you smile. Remind me to tell you the one about how I messed up with a turkey sandwich."

Lenny survived without any damage to his vital organs. Eventually, the prison changed the shaving devices from razor blades to shavers with batteries. Batteries could be swallowed too, of course. In a place of limited resources, most anything was fair game.

We Have Power

Seventeen men from the United Blood Nation gang housed in solitary confinement organized a protest action.[†] At a desig-

---

[†] Protest actions occurred frequently, about any number of issues—bad food, ignored requests, or any time inmates felt disrespected.

nated time, they stuffed sheets and shirts into their cell toilets. It flooded their housing unit and the floor beneath them.

The water was shut off. All the men stopped their yelling and banging against their doors except one man. He finally was placed in four-point restraints for twenty-four hours.

I visited him the next day. I brought written prayers to give to him that were a part of his Rastafarian faith. But he was banned from receiving any papers or books. So I talked to him through the trap window of his cell.

"You knew you couldn't win. Why'd you do that?" I asked.

"Because we're not going to take it anymore. They need to know we have power," he said.

A No Go

I was the one to make arrangements for an inmate to leave the prison when an immediate family member died. They couldn't go to the funeral, only the private viewing. In prison uniform and fully shackled, both wrists and ankles, the inmate was driven by car with two armed officers. Occasionally, an inmate wasn't approved, especially if he had an escape record, or if he was known for violence.

Sean desperately wanted to go to the viewing for his grandmother who raised him, but time was running out to make the arrangements. Since he was infraction free, his chances for approval seemed good. His record clearly stated that his grandmother raised him. It was all the verification needed.

"Still need more verification," my boss said, shuffling his papers without looking up from his desk. "Get a signed report card by his grandmother from his school days, or a legal document of guardianship."

Sean's family was at the funeral home completing final arrangements when I called. "Why didn't you tell us what was needed yesterday or even this morning?" his cousin asked. I explained with equal pain in my voice that I'd just gotten the request. He said he'd run back to the house and see what he could find.

Twenty pages of faxed documents arrived an hour later. Car deeds and insurance policies proved that he'd had the same address as his grandmother. I grabbed them and sprinted back to my boss's office. "Here's what they sent."

He flipped through the pages. "No report cards. No legal guardianship papers. So no go."

I pleaded that the majority of the families didn't have legal guardianship papers. They simply take the kids in. "Even I don't keep my kids' report cards," I said.

"Sorry," he said. "No can do. The regional office wants more proof. Policy changes."

"Today? Now?" I sensed my voice rising to match my frustration. "I've been doing this for ten years. We've never been asked for this kind of proof."

"You'll just have to call the family and tell them we're sorry."

I grabbed my boss's phone and gave them the bad news. The response was so loud I held the phone from my ear. "But she is his heart!" his cousin cried. "This is the only mother he's ever really known. I don't want to speak bad about my aunt, but she was no mother for Sean. In and out of prison too much. What else can I send you? I'll fax stuff all night long. I'll trade places with him. What do you want? Just let him come to the funeral home. Please let him come."

I apologized again and hung up the phone. "*Damn!* That was an awful thing we just did to this family," I said to my boss. "It was wrong, *so* wrong."

"He should've thought of all of this before he committed his crime," he responded flatly. I never knew what to do with statements like that. I huffed out his door and back to my office.

I threw myself into my chair. I reached in the candy jar on my desk and started firing peppermints against the walls. When my ammunition ran out, I crossed my arms and continued to fuel my anger. The transportation officer showed up at my door. He looked at the floor.

"Chap, do you know that you have peppermints all over your floor?"

"Yes, I do. My head exploded."

"We always wondered what was in your head," he said, hoping for a smile. "Guess that guy's not going to any funeral home."

"Guess not."

I thought about what I'd said to my boss and wished I'd used stronger profanity. Before I left for the day, I handed tissues to a broken-hearted grandson.

The next morning, one of the gatehouse officers asked a question out of the blue: "Hey, Chap, what do you think about this Gospel of Judas?"

I didn't know anything about that gospel. I searched for a theologically astute thing to say when all I could really think about was the betrayal of the day before. Before I could say anything, the clearance officer piped up, "Oh don't worry about that kind of thing. If you're in doubt, you can always fall back on love."

Well, that was better than anything I could have come up with. I knew I needed to remember those times when kindness seeped in instead of all the times when there was no love to fall back on. Just the week before, an officer was delayed in returning from a private viewing for an inmate's mother. "Traffic was terrible. But it was worth it. His brothers seemed to have a reconciliation. It was a blessing to see them come together."

One day I noticed an officer outside as I was coming into the prison. He asked if I could sit a minute. I noticed his red-rimmed and watery eyes.

"Don't tell anybody, but my wife and I are having some problems, bad problems. I started taking her for granted. I didn't give her what she needed. I love her. She's my rock. But it's not good now. We're going through the valley of the shadow of death, and I'm afraid. Only God can help us now. Can you pray for me?"

I assured him I would. "I've let this place get to me," he said. "I turned away from God. I come home hateful and tired. I need to get away from this place. It'll tear you up inside. If I could find another job today, I'd take it. This place is starting to bother my health, my mind, my spirit. It's taking its toll on me. And now I'm coming apart. I can't take it."

I prayed with him. Then we sat in silence looking at the grey canopy of clouds settling in on the mountain ridge.

A Reason for Everything

One blustery fall day, a dozen of us, staff and officers, stood in a semicircle, silently staring at the charred ground where an officer's car had burst into flames. He died there. On that spot. Friend and colleague. Ashes to ashes. A wreath was pushed into the ground, next to a lone scorched pine tree that marked the spot. It was a mystery how the accident happened. All that stood sentinel was that solitary pine tree, less than ten inches around. A prayer was offered. Clumps of toilet paper were passed around as tears were shed. "We don't know what the next moment will bring," one officer intoned. "Life or death. So let's be good to each other. Let's care about each other."

On the drive back, I told the officer, "You know, when nothing makes sense and my heart is stuck in my throat, I take walks in the woods. What do you do?"

"Well, last week we buried my cousin, killed by her husband. I tell myself that there is a reason for everything, even when I can't see it." We rode in silence the rest of the way.

Happy Birthday, Frederick

I was surprised when Frederick blurted out, "You know what? Today was the best birthday of my thirty-five years. Guys gave me honey buns and cups of soup and candy bars. Made me feel like some folks are glad that I was born. For the past sixteen years, I've spent my birthdays in prison. Most birthdays I'm sad because none of my family remembers me. But it didn't matter that I didn't get a card today. I felt happy all day long. In fact, I've felt blessed."

He said that when he was growing up there was only one time that his birthday was remembered. But I thought maybe part of his blessed feeling might be credited to the day before. It was the birthday of a man on Frederick's block who didn't have any money, so Frederick bought some things and asked the canteen man to give it anonymously to the other inmate. He said he was glad he could give something, knowing what it was like to be without anything.

I blew soap bubbles on Frederick and launched a wind-up toy birthday cake across my desk. That's a birthday celebration, prison style.

J.C.

J.C. took a break from his soap-opera viewing of *The Young and the Restless* to request a phone call to his mother in a nursing home. Set above sunken cheeks and a long grey beard, his sky-blue eyes were almost lost in the shadows that surrounded them. Spider tattoos were on every finger. He had five years down and fifteen to go on a second-degree murder charge.

He grew up malnourished in both body and soul. Meals in his home were cooked on a coal-burning stove, and food was scarce. School wasn't a priority, and J.C. never learned to read and write. When he was twelve years old, his dad "blew his brains out" playing Russian roulette in the living room while J.C. and his brother and sister were watching TV. His mother had told his dad to put the gun away, but they were both too drunk to do the right thing.

J.C.'s live-in girlfriend of fourteen years had been a passing-out alcoholic. He told me that she came at him many times with a knife when she was drunk, which was often. "Why didn't you leave her?" I asked him.

"Reckon I don't know," he said. "I loved her. I took care of her grandbaby. Wish I could do it all over again." He stroked his beard as he thought about it all. "As for choking her, I don't remember. I'm not a woman beater."

"I'm glad to hear it, J.C."

"I'm a thief, but not a murderer," he explained. "I didn't mean to kill her. I was trying to stop her." He looked up like his life was being projected on the ceiling. "Next thing I know she was asleep, and I couldn't wake her up. I called 911. Five days later they said she was brain-dead." When his girlfriend died, J.C.'s charge was changed from assault to murder.

Years ago he testified against his partner from his thieving days, and J.C. believed that people were out to get him—a fear that was not entirely unfounded. One day when he was coming back from chow, three guys threw him into a cell. One stood at the door while the other two went in, broke two ribs, and bruised and battered his eyes.

"No one put me here but myself," he admitted. "My mom cries a lot now. Last time I talked to her, we both cried." He sat for a while and then said, "Now you've heard the whole rigmarole." He got up to leave but stopped at the doorway and added, "Everybody's in a hurry. No one has time to listen. Thanks, Chap. I feel lighter."

Paul

Paul was being moved to a prison with a hospital wing, and we needed to quickly find a family member to sign a DNR (do not resuscitate) form. "You need to jump on it, Chap—*asap*. Call me back as soon as you can," my boss said briskly.

I searched Paul's records and called the three numbers listed for family. Each time I heard the audible dead end: *This number is no longer in service.* I looked through phone directories. Nothing.

I walked to the housing unit to see Paul in his cell. An officer accompanied me, opening the door as it buzzed and unlocked. He held the door and whispered, "Paul's not doing too good. He won't give you any trouble. Sometimes he gets really confused. We do what we can to help him." I often saw such kindness from officers when an inmate was extremely ill.

It was rare that I had reason to enter a cell. It felt intrusive to walk into a tiny space with only a toilet, sink, and bed. It was made worse by the fact that I'd not met Paul before and only just learned of his condition.

Some cells were made more inviting with family photos on the wall. But Paul's cell was barren, as stripped away as his life. His belongings looked sparse on the metal shelf, a few papers, shirts, pants. He sat on the edge of his neatly made up bed. One look at his emaciated body confirmed that he was gravely ill. His body was disintegrating. Staff members could not name aloud his illness because of policies on medical confidentiality, but it was likely that he was dying of complications from AIDS.

I waved my hand to get his attention. "Paul, it's good to see you today. How are you doing?" His thin body twitched as he raised his head, smiled, and assured me that he was doing well. "Getting better every day," he said. His sunken eyes and deeply creviced wrinkles made it difficult to believe that he was only forty-five years old. Prison had been his home since he was twenty.

Leaning over to meet his face, I told him that he would soon be taken to a new place that could take special care of him. His face softened. I asked him if he had a letter from his family. "Yes, ma'am." He reached for his Bible on the shelf, opened it to the middle and handed me a torn, coffee-stained letter. I held it gently and asked to read it. He nodded. It was a four-year-old letter from a niece. The ink was fading, but there were legible numbers for her mother and cousin. "Can I borrow this letter for a few minutes?" Again, he smiled and nodded. I returned to my office to call, but all the numbers were disconnected.

I walked back to the cell to return the letter. "Paul, thank you for letting me borrow this letter. Your niece wrote such wonderful things about you. She clearly loves you. Now before you go on your journey, let's pray together." He closed his eyes as I placed a hand on his shoulder. Then I became silent with uncertainty. I thought there should be other words to say in that moment, but they didn't come to me. The officer was holding the door. My boss was waiting for my call. I turned to leave saying the words, "God's peace to you, Paul."

Paul lifted his Bible above his head with shaky hands. In a clear, strong voice he prayed, "Thank you, God, for your many blessings. Thank you for looking down upon me and lifting me up when I've fallen down. Thank you for giving me your grace. Thank you for giving me your love. And now I pray the whole world gets a holda your love and ever'body lives in peace. In the name of Jesus, Amen."

Thanksgiving and blessing. Paul knew what the moment called for. As he laid his Bible on his lap, I tried to hold back my tears but failed. I opened my arms wide and gave him a hug. As I walked back through the cell door, the officer gave me a nod of approval. We both knew that hugs were against policy, of course.

Paul died a month later. No family member was found; no DNR was needed.

Superintendent Dan

Phone in one hand, cigarette in the other, Dan was the model of efficiency, nodding a welcome "yep" or "nope" to his staff and whatever prison problems we brought to him.

"Dan, how about an Easter egg roll for the inmates this year?" I'd tease.

"Nope, nope, nope," he'd say without looking up.

"Okay then, there's a great place out there for a petting zoo—and we already have a fence."

"Nope, nope, nope," he'd reply with a sideways grin.

He didn't even answer when I suggested that it was only fair for the Rastafarians to have a revival like the Christians. "We'd need a reggae band for that, of course," I said. He just grinned. I thought of him years later when, miraculously, we did get that reggae band for the Rastas.

Dan usually greeted me with his raised cigarette. "Chap, these things'll kill ya. I'm gonna stop. I swear I'm gonna stop one day."

I was in his office one afternoon with a complaint. There was a training video that showed the many ways that inmates manipulate the staff, and one example was about a female chaplain who was conned out of her pantyhose by a male inmate who then sold it to the highest bidder on his cellblock. It made me furious.

"There's only a handful of us female chaplains working in men's prisons," I lamented. "Staff already consider us naïve, and this doesn't help. After the video several officers asked me about my pantyhose. I blurted out *shit!* I told them that I didn't even wear pantyhose, and then I cussed some more. I thought you should hear this from me first. I apologize for my un-chaplain–like behavior and all the cussing."

Dan flipped his tie over his shoulder, laughing. "Oh, hell. I knew you had it in you. Nobody thinks you're an angel, you know."

One summer day, my Sunday afternoon ritual of stretching out on the sofa and reading the newspaper was interrupted by a phone call. It was rare to hear from the prison during my off hours, and when I did, it was never good news.

"Chap, we lost our superintendent today."

I couldn't believe what I was hearing. The voice on the other end repeated the news, "We lost Dan today," the assistant superintendent said.

"Heart attack?" I thought the smoking must have caught up with him.

"No, it looks like he took his own life."

Rumors were whispered through the prison halls to explain Dan's absences over the past year. It was no secret that he drank too much. He might have kept that fact hidden except for his DUI citations. His mother's death only a few weeks before his own was another possible factor.

I remembered a story Dan told from the time when he was deputized as an officer with the county sheriff. It was a domestic disturbance. Two officers had already been shot. Law enforcement swarmed in from three counties. When Dan arrived on the scene, he found one officer dead on the front porch. Another was badly wounded. Both were friends of his from childhood.

As Dan continued the story, cigarette smoke shrouded his face. The officers ran into the woods in all directions looking for the suspect, but it was Dan who found him. The man was sitting under a rock ledge, easily within firing range. Dan pointed his gun. "I could've shot him right then and there," he said. "But the guy had two guns on his lap while he lit up a cigarette."

"What kept you from pulling the trigger?" I asked.

"The man didn't have the gun in his hand. It wouldn't have been the right thing to do. Meeting one wrong with another one doesn't make things right." He stopped to stub out his cigarette. "Me and the other officers sure were criticized for not going ahead and killing that man. But you know what the sheriff said at the funeral? 'We brought him out alive. We're not murderers. That's what separates us from them.'"

Dan lit another cigarette and tried to clear his throat. He looked out the window and said, "I'm proud we performed our duties without letting emotions and anger control us."

I walked into the line-up room as the news about Dan's death was given to the officers awaiting their shift. I offered a prayer. The captain warned everyone to stay on their game given this "disturbance." Silently a hundred officers made their way to their posts. Later, in Dan's office, I wondered if anything could have kept him from pulling the trigger that morning.

The next day some staff members as well as inmates asked me, "Is he in hell for taking his own life?" I was ready to cuss again. Damn that misguided religious belief. Damn it. No, I said. He was in hell before he pulled the trigger. He's with a merciful God now.

One sergeant asked me, "He took the coward's way out, didn't he?" But then he paused and added, "I guess maybe it takes a brave man to put a gun to his mouth and pull the trigger."

People think what they will about it. I still think Dan died of a heart attack, a long, slow heart attack.

Maalik

I bent over to see a face through the opening in the narrow trap door of seg. "I'm scared," Maalik said. "Some officers threaten us. They tell us we better not eat the food 'cause it might be poisoned." He didn't think he could make it any longer. It was one week into the month-long fast of Ramadan, and his insides were stripped bare from fasting. He'd snapped at another inmate. With a snap back, they both landed in lock-up.

"I know they're just messin' with our minds," he said, "but I'm tired of this. You can't trust anybody."

I asked him how much longer before he could go home. "Four more years," he said. "I don't think I can make it. I'm sad. Sad about this place. Sad about my life. Sad about my own stupid actions that got me into this place. Sad about all the times I get called 'boy' and cussed out for nothin'. I'm tired, Chap. Tired of tryin'. Tired of being treated like I'm not human, like I'm not a man."

With a tilt of his head to the ceiling, tears pooled in his eyes. "Sorry, Chap. I don't know what's wrong with me. I usually keep it together."

I remembered a time when I was filled with despair and sorrow. I too had been fasting, and everything mangled and menacing came to the surface. I said to him what a wise pastor said to me in that moment: "Maalik, you've been fasting. The lid is off. Every feeling in you is exposed. Your anger and hurt and grief are all there to see, and it's not easy to look at them. But go ahead and look. Stare 'em down. It'll leave its mark, but it won't destroy you. You're going to make it. Guard your soul. There's strength in you to get to the other side of this.

Right now, why don't you just rest. I'll be back tomorrow to check on you."

The next morning I went to his cell and found him smiling. "What happened to you?" I asked.

"I don't know exactly. But last night I was cryin' like a baby. And the guy in the next cell started bangin' on the wall sayin', 'Hey, man, you all right?' So I said, 'Yeah, man. I think I'm gonna make it.' Then the guy started poundin' harder and harder on the wall sayin', 'You're gonna make it, man. You're gonna make it.' I started laughin' and cryin' at the same time. I yelled, 'I'm gonna make it!' Then I pounded on the wall back at him and said, 'Man, you're gonna make it! You're gonna make it!' I don't know how long we went on like that, but it was long enough for me to start believin' it."

My sister told me that on a lark she'd seen a palm reader at a street fair. "Good news," she said. "Turns out I've got not one but *two* angels looking after me. And not to worry, she told me, they're coming—they're just *delayed.*"

I know the guys often felt that but more keenly—like there were no angels, never had been, not even delayed ones. What we say holds the most meaning for us—family, someone to love, meaningful work—these are laid as sacrifices on the altar of prison. "Two times I listen for my name to be called," Chester told me. "Mail call and visitation. My life isn't meaningless without it, but it makes a difference. My grandkids don't know their Paw Paw. I don't want to be forgotten. But I'm going to be a man of God, and you can become a man of God anywhere."

For those who felt forgotten, like their lives mattered to no one, "not worth a bullet in the barrel" as one inmate put it—for those men, the words of old gospel songs held deep meaning. Simple, plaintive, the hymn they liked best,

the one that ended many of the chapel services, came as
little surprise.

> *Trusting only in Thy merit,*
> *Would I seek Thy face;*
> *Heal my wounded, broken spirit,*
> *Save me by Thy grace.*
>
> *Pass me not, O gentle Savior,*
> *Hear my humble cry;*
> *While on others Thou art calling,*
> *Do not pass me by.*

11

This World Is Not My Home

At the end of the day, it isn't where I came from.
Maybe home is somewhere
I'm going and never have been before.

—Warsan Shire

Two nurses with red-stained towels draped across their arms were handing fresh white ones to the man in the open-barred cell. He wouldn't let them near him. Pacing back and forth, he was only in a pink paper skirt wrapped at the waist—the wardrobe for a man on suicide watch. Dark red blotches stained the paper. He'd cut himself—slashes ran across one arm and straight down his abdomen. I stopped to see if I knew the inmate—a handsome man with tightly cropped hair—but I didn't.

A psychologist showed up during the towel exchange. The assessment was complete. "He's fine. Just wants off this camp. Just wants some attention."

Attention he was getting. A dozen faces were staring through their own cell windows watching. Some slammed their hands against their door in a drumbeat of solidarity. The captain moved toward him and said, "Listen, we've got to get the other razors from you. Can you help us out here?"

A thundering *no!* was heard as the pacing continued. I asked a nurse about the razors. "He claims he's got four more wrapped in plastic and stuck up his behind, but who knows?"

The captain tried again. "If you have a complaint about things here, I want to hear it."

Silence.

The doctor arrived. His outstretched arms reached through the bars as he calmly said, "Son, what's your name?"

"It don't matter."

"It does matter. What do you like to be called?"

"Rift."

"Well, Rift, I'm your doctor. I'm here to help you."

"No, you're not. Nobody's here to help me. Nobody'll listen to me."

"Rift, I have all the time you need. I'm here to listen."

"No you're not. You're just like all the rest. I'm gonna kill myself today, or I'm gonna make you all do it for me because I'll fight ya."

The doctor patiently explained that that wasn't going to happen, that he was there to help and wanted to know what the problem was.

"Officers are tryin' to get me. They trip me up, call me names. Racists. All of 'em racists. I'm a man, and I ain't gonna take it anymore. The power's all in their hands. They get all the say. I got no power. Nothing's gonna change. They win every time."

"That's serious. I'm glad you told me," he replied in measured tones. "But right now we need to get you safe. So can you give us the razors?"

"No, I got nothin' more to say to you. Today's my last day alive, I swear!"

The captain stepped closer to the cell. "These are serious accusations, Rift, and if any of my officers are doing these things, I want to know about it. But we can't address them if we're spending all our time with you in a crisis."

Rift walked back and forth without another word.

As the staff moved to another room to confer, I stepped closer to the bars and asked if I could offer a prayer.

"A prayer?" He spit on the ground. "What do I need a prayer for?"

"You got kids?"

"Yeah, three. What they got to do with anything?"

"Everything. Could you tell me about them? How old are they? What do they like to do? This day is about them, too."

"I don't need no chaplain. You can get outta here now."

He picked up his pace, head down, shaking it back and forth. From my side of the bars, I joined him, pacing my steps in sync with his.

"Hey, did you hear that the Braves beat the Cowboys?" I asked.

His feet halted and his eyes rose to meet mine. "You crazy? Those ain't even the same kinda teams. You're confused."

"Yep. That's me. Crazy and confused. Get called that a lot."

He repeated that he didn't need a chaplain and told me to leave. With that he picked up the pace on his narrow switchback trail. I decided he might be right. He didn't want a chaplain, or anyone, for that matter—not even himself. Just as I walked away, the captain and the doctor returned with a plan. Rift was transported to a prison facility that could offer medical and psychiatric treatment. His cuts were not life-threatening, nor was it the first time he'd cut himself. It probably wouldn't be the last either. But it sickened me that this young man, like so many others in prison, inflicted pain on his body, as if outward scars vivified the inward ones.

I never saw him again. But I heard that he stayed alive.

Roland

Roland was a tall, thin inmate who walked like a marionette, loosely hinged at the joints. He was only sixteen when he was sent to prison for assault with a deadly weapon. Nine years didn't alter his teenage gait or demeanor. Folding into a chair, he blurted, "I'm desperate to talk to a chaplain about the female officer on my block." With my own hunches about "desperate," I advised him to be very careful in choosing his words with me.

"Chap, a female officer on my block is coming on to me."

Oh dear, I thought, and so it begins. I told him I doubted it, that he was misinterpreting her actions.

"No, I swear. She comes up close to me and wants me to touch her."

"Okay, that's enough about that. All you need to do is act responsibly and walk away," I said, reminding him that he was getting out in a few years and not to mess up his record.

"Hey, I wouldn't even be here if I'd had a better partner."

"What do you mean a better partner? Are you blaming a girlfriend for your crime?"

"No, I mean my crime partner, not a girl. My partner and I were using drugs and the drug dealer wasn't doing right by us, so we decided to scare him a little. So we tied him up and put him in the trunk of the car to take him for a little ride. But then my partner was speeding, and a police car pulled us over. My partner shoulda never stopped. I'd've kept on going. How stupid is that?"

"Stupid started long before the car was pulled over," I said.

DJ

I was curious to know what DJ thought about the inauguration of our first black president. He slung his dreads around with a dip of his neck and groaned, "How do you get excited about something that should've been happening all along? When slaves were emancipated, what kind of emancipation was that?" Then he went on to tell me of a guy he was talking to in medical, a white guy who killed another white guy. He got eighteen years. When DJ told him that his sentence was life without parole, without missing a beat, the guy said, "so you killed a white guy, huh?"

"Everybody knows that kind of truth, Chap. I had no weapon and no intention of killing anybody. And that white guy brutally killed the man. So, yeah, I'm glad that Obama is president. It's good, but will change come for a man like me? Not anytime soon. Maybe never."

We All Got Pain, Man

It was Tuesday night writing group. All ten members of the group sat in the circle. They had written their reflections on *Freedom Writers*, a movie depicting the true story of a teacher who encouraged her "at risk" students to write about their lives.

Emilio said that he wanted to go first since he was from South Central L.A. and could speak directly about the authenticity of the movie. I guess he did know a thing or two—his mom shot his dad when Emilio was just nine years old. That's when he and his brother joined a gang that became their family. At twelve, he shot a man and then a few more after that, including one he thought had raped his mom. By the time he moved to North Carolina, he'd seen more violence than anyone should in a lifetime. "I've been in prison here since I was seventeen," he told me. "Gangs here are nothing. Prisons here are nothing. This is day care."

Emilio's fast-paced street talk sounded like a foreign language. He said that he was in the writing group because this lady (pointing to me) asked him to come up to her office. "Then she wanted to know why so many staff were saying my name," he said. "What is there to be afraid of from you? she asked me. Next thing I know, I'm tellin' her my story."

He laughed and then told the group the whole story, punctuated by the refrain, "No one can feel my pain. No one."

Another member of the group stopped him. "Man, if you think that no one can feel your pain, then you back yourself into a corner, and you make yourself alone, and then you start feeling bitter inside, and you can't get out of that cause you think that you're the only one in the world who has as hard a pain as you got. Maybe no one's gone through your pain, but all of us hurt. And the only way to get through the hurt is to feel like there're others like you who hurt. Man, we're in this hurtin' life together, and we gotta pull alongside each other. It makes it better to know you ain't the only one. My mom was raped, too. I was just a little kid. Five years old. I heard her screamin'. I couldn't do nothin' about it. But you got your face back. I couldn't do that. I was too little. We all got pain, man. We all got pain. Stop thinkin' you're so special."

Last Day for Officer

Sunday noon. I breezed through segregation to tell an inmate happy news of his sister's new baby. As I was leaving the floor, I stuck my head in the break room where three officers were setting food on the table for their lunch. I expected a simple "okay" when I asked how it was going, but Officer Wilkes had some things on his mind.

"It's my last day. Four years of this place is more than enough. I'm joining the army. I'll start at Fort Benning next week. Then to Iraq for eighteen months. I'll get a $30,000 bonus for joining the infantry for overseas assignment."

"Iraq?"

"I can handle it," he said. "I'll buy some more shields. The vests the army gives you can just repel shrapnel. So I'll buy a vest that can repel bullets. It costs $1,000. I'll also get a metal shield for the front and back, $900 each."

"What's your feeling about the war?"

"Oh, I'm against it. I don't think we should be there. But when I go, I'll do everything I can to protect the people in our uniforms."

"So your best option for leaving the prison is to join the army?" I asked.

"Yeah. You can't get ahead in this system. We're the lowest of the low in terms of state employees. Nobody cares about us, because nobody cares about inmates. The only thing people care about is keeping these guys away from society. There aren't enough programs for them. There is 85 percent recidivism rate. We release some guys to homeless shelters. They have it better in here than they do out there. And when they closed a lot of the mental health places in the state, where do you think they went? Here. So they learn to live in this environment, and they can't make it anywhere else. And nobody cares about them or us. Nobody. It's not going to change. So, I'm going where I have a chance. The army can give me a chance for an education and train me. I can see the world and get a promotion based on my merit. Promotions in here? All based on who you know, not what you know. I can say this because it's my last day."

He kept rolling out his reasons for his decision. "This is a house of cards. It's dangerous. You got times when a guy is cornered and he knows he's beat, but he keeps on fighting. You wanna know why?" Of course, I wanted to know why.

"To save face," he said. "He doesn't want to be seen as a coward. He wants to be able to say that he got some licks in, and he got that officer good. Even when there are six officers from the PERT team [Prison Emergency Response Team] with shields, pepper spray, and helmets, sometimes an inmate will still fight back knowing good and well that he won't win. It's all about saving face. Guys will risk their life for it."

He put a dish of baked beans on the table. "My mom made these. She puts brown sugar and pork in it. She makes the best. You want to join us for lunch?"

I sat down to a table of baked beans, hot dogs, slaw, potato chips, and chili sauce. The officers ate quickly before returning to their post, offering handshakes and a "Good luck, man" on their way out.

Officer Wilkes ate slowly, savoring the beans. "My mom makes the best beans in the world, doesn't she? I'm going to miss her cooking."

A Well-disguised System of Control

When one of the officers badgered an inmate about buttoning his shirt, I asked him why he didn't just button it. He told me it was his way of "bucking." "They're killing our spirits, Chap, one button at a time."

"You don't need to spend time in prison," Howard Moody wrote, "to see that what we have is not a criminal *justice* system but a criminal *control* system." Since the early 1960s, Moody, the longtime minister at Judson Memorial Church in New York City, advocated passionately for drug policy reform and against mass incarceration and its underlying injustice to marginalized people. "And the morally reprehensible thing," he continued, "is that it institutionalizes hopelessness. . . . As for the prisons and the criminal control system, we would have to sacrifice our desire for punishment which derives from vengeance—vengeance that makes prisons into charnel-houses of human degradation, guaranteed to turn out bitter and resentful citizens."*

This wasn't news to me. I just never imagined being in a place where so many were trapped "with their backs against the wall," as Howard Thurman put it, and many unjustly because of poor legal representation or punitive drug laws unevenly applied across racial and economic lines. I thought about the captain's instruction for counting—to line them up against the wall, but don't look them in the eye. It seemed like I was living in a country that started doing that to a whole community of people, unwilling to see the faces of those we'd imprisoned or hear their stories. I'll never forget what "Bear" said to me one day—"A lot of us in here are *nobodies-you'd-notice* from a place called *nowhere-special* and got stuck in a spot called *nobody-cares.*"

A poem from an inmate . . .

Fly

Imagine yourself away from the monotonous routine of the day,
away from whatever problems or troubles that vex you and
envision the azure skies opening up before you as
you take flight.
Let the whispering wind revitalize your
spirit as it sweeps over you and through you all the way
down to the very shimmer of
your soul. Let it sink so far down within you that it emanates
from your skin like sweat.

---

* Howard Moody, "Prisons and Ghettos: The Nurturing of Hopelessness," sermon for Judson Memorial Church, New York, New York, October 27, 1991.

*When you awake perhaps wrongs may not have been rectified
and you
still may have to reiterate your points to those who are
determined to make you dull. . .
but as you face them you
can smile coyly for you and I know
we can fly.*

12

Treading Underfoot,
Casting into the Sea

The weak can never forgive.
Forgiveness is the attribute of the strong.

—Mahatma Gandhi

"We're all saints and sinners," Monk, our volunteer, told the writing group one night. "Knowing my own guilt in the failings of my life gives me more room to forgive others. I have plenty that I need to forgive myself for."

Forgiveness was a tough topic. It was a complicated brew of parental failings, poor choices, consequences of addiction, lives broken or brutally snuffed out. For many, it was a long list of people to forgive, people from whom they needed forgiveness, and for some the most difficult— forgiving themselves. The guys were wildly divergent in their opinions—jumping up and yelling.

Monk got their attention again when he said in his soft, easy way, "Well, I've known Chap a long time. I've known her to be violent, self-righteous, and arrogant. I think that she's able to forgive because she knows about her own failings."

You can bet they wanted a story about that.

"Aw, you already know some of those stories," Monk continued. "Remember when George said, 'Chap's a cat,' she purrs with warmth and acceptance, but can, without notice, hiss and show her claws at the very scent of manipulation? She's tough, but I know sometimes things around here get to her. She wishes she'd said something differently, responded differently. Then again, we all do, don't we?"

The men started wondering about their victims and their own forgiveness.

One man read his piece about forgiveness, and said that he didn't think he'd ever know enough forgiveness for the things he'd done. He ended his essay with the sobering words that many felt—"I think I'll have to carry my guilt to my grave."

As we walked out of the prison that night, Monk said to me, "After all our training and experience, we're still humbled by groups and can't begin to figure them out. I'm wondering how we got to be so fortunate to witness this kind of depth of honesty about forgiveness. We've discussed forgiveness so many times in church circles but never was there such passion, such longing to know if it's real." He paused in the parking lot and summed things up. "You know, for those men, the truth of forgiveness really is life or death."

A Simple Cup of Cold Water

Monk was right. I was haunted by some things I'd said and done at the prison. During the annual field day, the inmates competed in the summer heat in basketball games, relay races, and other athletic events. Then their fruit punch ran out. While the staff had a full cooler of drinks in the shaded comfort, thirsty inmates lined up at a water fountain under the blazing sun.

Jim watched the competition from the sideline in his wheelchair, his permanent injury the result of a drug-related gunshot wound. The water fountain was out of reach for him, so he wheeled over to the staff tent and asked if he could have a cup of water. They said no.

Then he came to me. "Chap, I can't reach the water fountain," he said.

I said I couldn't help. I looked right at Jim and said I couldn't help.

I still agonize as I write those words. Giving a cup of cold water—what could be more simple, more humane, more *biblical*. But I chose to be a rules follower. I wanted to be a team player that staff and officers could trust. And perhaps worst of all, I was just trying to keep a job I desperately needed.

After a sleepless night, I arrived at the prison with the firm resolve to make amends. When Jim saw me in his housing unit, he worried that I was "the angel of death" with bad news about his family. Instead I apologized for not offering water to him on the yard. He shook his head and said in exasperation, "Chap, this ain't about you. This whole damn mess ain't about you."

It was all a great big mess. I think to myself quite often, against my will as it were. But today I suddenly wondered why I used the word mess in the first place. It is so much hot air and doesn't make things any better.

These are the words of Etty Hillesum from the book, *An Interrupted Life: The Diaries of Etty Hillesum 1941–1943*. I kept this small paperback on my desk at the prison, held together by a rubber band, the cover gone, the pages curled and yellowed. Each time I held it I thought I should buy a new copy, but the passages I frequented were so clearly marked that I didn't want to part with it.

There's no adequate way to explain my sense of connection to Etty since I'd never known anything close to her suffering. A Dutch Jew who died in Auschwitz at the age of twenty-nine, her diaries examined her "tempestuous, havoc-ridden world" with honesty and compassion. As Etty's outer world diminished by oppressive and inhumane treatment, her inner world expanded with a luminous humanity. "The sky within me is as wide as the one stretching above my head," she wrote. On the days when I couldn't see the sky, when my sight was blocked by numbness and indifference, I reached for her book, and Etty became my teacher.

"A large group of us were crowded into the Gestapo hall," she wrote, "and at that moment the circumstances of all our lives were the same. All of us occupied the same space, the men behind the desk no less than those about to be questioned. What distinguished each of us was only our inner attitude." The degradation and diminishment of interactions in prison became no more alien to me than what Etty witnessed. What became more noticeable, more breathtaking, were people who displayed an inner freedom that interrupted the gloom, transforming hatred to love, withdrawal to engagement, hopelessness to hope.

I used one of Etty's prayers so often that it became a portable candle I lit at the altar of miseries. "Dear God, these are anxious times . . . I shall try to help You, God, to stop my strength ebbing away, though I cannot vouch for it in advance. But one thing is becoming increasingly clear to me: that You cannot help us, that we must help You to help ourselves. And that is all we can manage these days and also all that really matters: that we safeguard that little piece of You, God, in ourselves. And perhaps in others as well."

Etty's brave determination to defend God's dwelling place within us fortified me. She saw the worst that humans could do to each other, hoping that a kinder generation could emerge. "The most depressing thing of all is that the mental horizon of all the people I work with is so narrow," she wrote about her forced labor in a concentration camp office. "They don't even suffer deep down. They just hate and blind themselves to their own pettiness, they are still ambitious to get on, it is all a great big, dirty mess and there are moments when I would like to lay my head down on my typewriter and say in despair, 'I can't go on like this.' But I do go on, learning more about people all the time."

Trent

"I'm sure you've already looked up my record," Trent said without a hint of emotion. He sat unusually straight. His frosty pale eyes blinked often. His broad shoulders and wide neck reminded me of a football player. I told him I knew he was thirty years old and convicted on drug charges—and that what surprised me was that he went to college, a rarity among inmates.

Trent told me he wanted to talk about "God-stuff" with somebody who knew about that sort of thing. He explained that he robbed to support a cocaine habit but never hurt anybody and was two years clean. In his seven years left in prison, he wanted "to work on his insides."

"First of all," he said, "I don't want you to tell me I'm forgiven," knocking out one of the main things I knew about God-stuff. "I want to know how to pay for my crime. I have a conscience. I can't tell the D.A. about all the crimes I've committed because I've done a lot and I'd be in for life. I can't go to my victims and tell them I'm sorry that I scared them—

there's too many of them. So this is what I want to know. What can I do so that I'm not looking over my shoulder and remembering all the terrible things I did and feeling guilty about it?"

I knew that place: that bit of real estate in your mind that stubbornly won't be sold to mercy and letting go. I pushed words around in my mind like food on a plate, looking for something to offer. Wasn't the point of prison to pay for his crime? But guilt? That ghost haunts for a lifetime.

I met his gaze and said, "Trent, truth is, I hope you do look over your shoulder from time to time. Those glances keep you human and merciful. You want to make amends? Live for the good."

His face registered no response. "I'm still going to find a way to pay it all back," he said as he stood to leave.

"That's good God-stuff, Trent," I said, pondering how I could navigate a similar course.

Dixon

Dixon was ready for a change. He said the devil was after his soul, and he felt like he was being chased down. "Chap, I want Jesus to come into my heart, just like he did when I was a little boy."

"And how was that, Dixon?"

"He came as a warm light inside of me. He lived inside me. I felt good. I felt loved. I felt free. Back when Jesus was inside me, that light in my heart gave me peace. What do I need to do to get Jesus back? I think it's too late. I've committed too many sins. I've hurt too many people. I hurt my parents something awful, and now they're dead, and I can't fix anything."

I reminded Dixon of the prayers of the Psalmist: *God, you know my crimes and my sins have not been hidden from you* (Psalm

51:3). *God hears the needy and does not despise those who are prisoners . . .* (Psalm 69:33).

I added the major words on forgiveness from the minor prophet Micah: *You will again have compassion on us; you will tread our sins underfoot and cast all our sins into the depths of the sea* (Micah 7:19). What an amazing thought—that whatever awful we've done can be trampled upon or sent out to sink in the sea.

Evan

The documentary film *The Power of Forgiveness* tells the story of acts of extraordinary forgiveness in response to horrific wrongs. After watching it, Evan was silent for a week. He then came to me and said he wanted to tell his story in chapel.

That's how I came to be standing next to him one Sunday, a pair of scissors slipped into my jacket sleeve out of sight. He adjusted the state-issued bug-eyed glasses on his broad face and read from a folded paper. "I'm halfway through my prison time. Eight down, eight to go," he said calmly. "Some of you know my situation and why I've been growing my hair long." His greying, waist-length hair was pulled back neatly into a ponytail. "I've kept it to remember my girlfriend. She loved my hair, brushed it every day."

Evan described the night of the cookout that included drinking, eating, and guitar playing. His girlfriend, Ginger, intended to drive home, but since she wasn't feeling well, Evan drove. The car crashed when he swerved to miss a dog. Ginger was killed in the accident. It was his intoxication that landed him in prison.

"I have a card from her best friend saying that she will take my ponytail to where Ginger's ashes are so that the birds can make nests with it." Without looking up, he continued. "If I've been short with you, I apologize and pray for your forgiveness and understanding. I've been tormenting innocent people with my own spirit of depression. Do I need Ginger's forgiveness now? I don't think so. I believe she forgave me a long time ago. Do I need her best friend's forgiveness? No, she's forgiven me, too. Do I need God's forgiveness? I believe that He also has forgiven me. Do I need God's guidance? Absolutely!

"So, it seems that God's guidance is showing me through this rough time that I need to forgive myself. If I don't, this circle will continue to expand and become an even heavier burden to bear. True forgiveness is a tough thing. I must first understand why I need this precious gift, and in my heart, I must know when to give it. I must also know in my heart when to receive it. I believe that now is the time to forgive myself."

Evan turned to me. I handed him the scissors. His ponytail draped on his shoulder as he snipped it away. Holding it high above his head, he smiled as everyone in the room stood, clapping and cheering. The choir swayed as they sang, "Amen, amen, amen . . ."

Sarge Makes a Visit

"Is this an approved color?" Sarge asked, waving a Rastafarian knit cap over my desk.

"No, Sarge, powder blue is not approved for Rasta prayer crowns, but I think it'd look good on you."

He rolled his eyes. This sergeant had a reputation for being the enforcer, aided by his sturdy build and booming voice. He turned to leave as quickly as he'd arrived. But as his hand reached the doorknob, he paused, "Chap, you got a minute?"

"Sure, Sarge."

"Everything I've ever cared about I lost from this job. I may not finish my career here. I'm looking at options. This job can't give me anything that matters. It prevents you from being a Christian. It pushes you the other way."

I told him we all feel pushed the other way at times; he was right, it was a tough place to be.

He leaned his head back, like an answer was written on the ceiling. "While I was standing in Master Control this morning, I looked at all those men coming to the chow hall and thought to myself, God loves them. God loves every one of them even though they messed up. Their wrong is a criminal wrong, but God forgives them. I've done a lot of things I regret in my life. Guess I'm looking for forgiveness, too."

Without waiting for a response from me, he walked out the door, dust particles following him in the sliver of sunlight from the window.

13

Another Kind of Force

Ours is not the task of fixing the entire world all at once,
but of stretching out to mend the part of the world
that is within our reach. Any small, calm thing that one soul
can do to help another soul, to assist some portion
of this poor suffering world, will help immensely.

—Clarissa Pinkola Estes

I stared at the magazine photo of the young girl. The year was 1963. I was twelve years old. We were born the same year, 1951. She had a coat with a Peter Pan collar, just like me. She had short, curly bangs, just like me. She sang in her Baptist church choir, just like me. But her skin color was not like me. A bomb had killed her and three other girls while they prepared for Sunday morning worship. Her name was Denise McNair.

As a good Baptist girl, I was taught to read my Bible daily and say my prayers. Every night that fall, I'd open my Bible and see the picture of Denise I'd nestled there. I held it between folded hands and asked God to stop the bombs that killed young girls and show me a way to help.

Days passed and I cut out more pictures of the violence and added them to my nightly ritual. There were plenty of them from earlier that spring in 1963: the guns, the whips, the fire hoses, the dogs, the bombs, the angry faces. They all chronicled the hatred. I spread them out on my bed. I couldn't make sense of it.

I wrote to the president of the United States, twelve pages in my best handwriting with my favorite blue cartridge ink pen. I wanted him to know that we were all created equal and God's message of love was that we didn't need to fight. The letter ended with "Mr. President, if you need any help with getting this message out, I'm available. You can reach me at DI8-1834 or you can write to me on Lanshire Drive in Dallas, Texas." I addressed the envelope to President Kennedy at the White House and placed it in the mailbox.

With each nightly prayer, my fantasy increased. I imagined the president contacting me, pleased with my offer. I pictured myself speaking in school auditoriums, in church halls and sanctuaries, and even in stadiums. But weeks passed and no invitation arrived.

On November 22, 1963, President Kennedy visited my hometown. The television monitor in my seventh-grade classroom showed the President and First Lady as they walked off Air Force One and into the motorcade. A short time later we heard the wobbly voice of the principal, "Boys and girls, the President of the United States has been shot. You will all go home now."

I joined my parents, my brothers, and sister in our den, huddled in front of the television as we listened to the horrifying news of the assassination. We sat in silence until my mother picked up an envelope and said, "Nancy, you got a letter today. It's from the White House."

I ran to my room to open the letter alone and read these words: "The President wants me to thank you for your letter. He and this Administration are dedicated to taking every necessary and proper step to end discrimination in all parts of our national life. . . . He appreciates your public spirit and concern for our national principles. . . . Your constructive leadership in this will be important, now and in the years to come." It was signed by Lee C. White, Assistant Special Counsel to the President.

For an impressionable twelve-year-old, the letter on that fateful day was enough to make a vow to God to be a peacemaker—or as I later learned from the teachings of Jesus, to find "a third way." Young Denise McNair would be my patron saint, if Baptists could have saints.

The Lieutenant

My office door was propped open to hear the choir members practicing. The call for chow was minutes away. One more verse of "I've Got Peace Like a River" and I'd have some peaceful moments to myself. But then an explosive voice rose above the chorus: "You shouldn't be in the choir. You don't know how to sing worth shit. White people got no feel for it."

I ran out of my office. "Choir is over today!" I shouted. "Leave. All of you leave *now!*"

They ignored me, so I jumped on a chair and yelled louder. I watched the lousy singer shove the instigator.

I raced back into my office and called for help. Seconds later the lieutenant and three officers arrived. "Back away! Hands up! *Now!*" The fighters were pulled apart while the other choir members scattered like ants to the corners of the room. Handcuffs were slapped on the offending parties. Within minutes the chapel was emptied and restored to calm.

I sank like an anchor in my chair. My hands wouldn't stop shaking. It was nothing more than a schoolyard brawl, I told myself. Teachers see this every day, I reasoned. Staff go home in one piece usually, I assured myself.

Over the years I've tried to practice nonviolent resistance, attending multiple trainings and workshops. But in the confines of quick tempers and sudden assaults, my training seemed limp and naïve.

I tried to center myself with slow breaths. Closing my eyes, I thought about riverbanks where the healing balm of the jewelweed plant grows right alongside poison ivy—the danger and its antidote, side by side. I promised myself that I wouldn't be stupid about the dangers, but I wasn't going to buckle to fear either.

I reached into the arsenal of chocolate in my bottom drawer. As I popped a few M&M's in my mouth, the lieutenant appeared at my office door. He offered no greeting, no recap of the event. He simply pointed his finger at me and said, "You don't like it, but you need me. And I don't like it, but I need you."

I downed my candies like pills. "Yes, Lieutenant," I sputtered. "That's true. I depend on you all for safety and security. But what do you need me for?"

"I need you to keep me from using undue physical force. I need you to teach me another kind of force." With his pronouncement hanging mid-air, he left.

Another kind of force? I could hardly believe what I heard. But I knew I had my work cut out for me.

Hide and Seek

To be sure an assault wasn't gang related, a full-scale search for weapons by PERT (Prison Emergency Response Team) was launched—seventy officers deployed from prisons all over the region. Adding to their numbers were about sixty more certified staff members from our prison. They marched single file through sliding doors to their destination, the housing units.

I asked a captain why there were so many officers at one time. "Show of force," he said. "We've gotta show 'em who's in control."

Teams of twenty or thirty officers swarmed a cellblock and upturned every possible hiding place for a weapon. I wasn't certified, but I wanted to be present for staff and inmates alike. There I stood, sentinel at the doorway of a cellblock. Sometimes I could be useful—interpreting whether an item was approved by religious policy. I was known to be able to save the prison from religious contraband, like a Native American leather pipe wrap, a Buddhist chiming bell, a Wiccan wooden chalice, or a cross made valuable in gold or silver.

Officers worked both tiers of the block at the same time, cell by cell. Each inmate was cuffed behind his back and placed in a plastic chair outside his room while it was being searched. He wore his undershorts so that all of his clothing could be examined. Papers were shuffled, books tossed, photos scattered. Flashlight beams darted under bedframes and around toilets. Trash heaps of forbidden items piled onto the floors. Too many books, magazines, or batteries were common alongside random things like a rabbit foot, a dream-catcher, or a strand of plastic beads. Once his room was searched, each man carried his mattress through a metal detector. Some were too old or infirm to manage it on their own and were assisted by staff. The effort took hours to complete.

At the end of that day, no weapons were found. I asked the captain, "If weapons had been found, what would prevent them from making more tomorrow?"

"Nothing. It's a game we play. Hide and seek. And would you believe that the only time I saw someone killed was when an inmate your size stabbed an inmate my size with a ballpoint pen?"

The Mentor

It was an unusually quiet morning, giving me no excuse for further procrastination on updates for the standard operating procedures manual on religious services. I was grateful for the interruption in that tedious work when Mr. Gustafson—"Mr. G"— a woodshop teacher, popped in, saying, "got a minute?" With a ready smile, he was the kind of person you hoped to see regularly in the dreary halls of the prison.

Pushing his glasses on top of his bald head, he said, "Can I ask you? Do you see your work here as a job or a calling?"

"Definitely a calling," I said.

"So how do you keep on doing it day after day? Do we make any difference at all? Is the system totally broken? Do you ever lose sleep over things here?" He pulled his glasses from his head and held them open.

"Sometimes." I decided not to tell him I take a sleeping pill. "Anything keeping you up at night?"

"Let me tell you a story. There was an inmate named Sam who had real talent. I saw the potential in him. I gave him opportunities to make things, to use his creativity over in the shop. He did a great job. He was dependable, trustworthy, and never got into trouble. I thought we'd done great in preparing him for a job after prison. When he got out, he got a good job. His boss was great—a person who gave him a second chance and a good salary. Then Sam blew it. He didn't report to work for a week. The business discovered they were missing some money. He broke into a car and stole some stuff. He ended up back in jail."

He stopped and fiddled with his glasses. "Now I'm wondering how I failed him. You see, when something like that happens, I look in the mirror and question myself. I ask what could I have done better? How could I have helped him more? I tell staff that these men need a chance, and we can give it to them. I tell them to look at the men with possibility and encourage them. But when something like this happens, they come and say, 'See what happened to your boy? Just nothing but a convict.'"

"But he wasn't 'my boy'," he continued. "I tried to help him, but this has shaken my foundation. It has shaken my faith. Sam had so much promise. Now I can't sleep at night thinking I failed."

"But you didn't fail him," I said softly. "You gave the very best of who you are. You gave him your faith in him. Sam wasn't ready to have faith in himself. Maybe he got overwhelmed. Maybe he'd lived here too long, with all the rules and decisions laid out for him. Maybe the choices were too many, and he wasn't up to the task. Maybe pressures on him just overtook him. Who knows? We can only imagine. But you didn't fail him."

"But I don't feel like I'm making a difference. What's the point in life if we don't try to do that? I want to see success.

If I don't figure it out, I don't know how to keep giving hope to these guys."

I told him that being humane and hopeful is a miracle and that hope poured out of him naturally, that it was a gift that some men would catch, though others might not.

"You're making a big difference, Mr. G," I said. "And you've made a difference in me today by telling me that story."

A Merciful Surprise

As I was writing up a stack of counseling memos, Michael came in to say he'd finished cleaning up after all the services. This was Michael the murderer, the one who was against female preachers, the one who only worked in the chapel because it was one of the better jobs on campus.

I thought he was just letting me know he was leaving when I noticed he was still standing at my door. "I gotta tell you something, Chap." He started crying, got embarrassed, and walked away. Then he came back and said, "I really appreciate you. I've been in prison for ten years and I don't get treated like a human being very much. And when you're in for this long, you start appreciating the little things. I appreciate all the little things you do, like a smile and a hello. And . . . I don't know how to say this because I don't want you to take it the wrong way, but I appreciate being around a woman like you. I respect you. I've learned a lot about God just from being around you. And I don't want you to think I am thinking about you in a weird way, but I haven't had a woman in my life like you. And, I'm changing. I don't know all the ways, but I'm changing. You've blessed me. And I want to thank you. That's all I got to say."

He darted back out the door.

The Fast Friend

Ralph was a smiling, easy-going inmate who attended services and sang in the choir. He was a pillar of religious conversion, as long as he stayed in the chapel. Outside of it, every perceived slight was cause for a fistfight. After fifteen years in prison, he told me that he was getting too old to fight all the time. "I'm no match for these young guys coming into prison now." Whether by conviction or weariness, he wanted to rein in his temper. With a forty-five year sentence and a decent record, that meant he could be released when he was seventy-five years old.

But at the end of one prayer service, he lost it. One of the guys just playfully tried to reach a pen out of Ralph's shirt pocket. "Don't do that, man! Don't ever touch me!" he yelled as he clutched his pocket.

I sent them packing, relieved that palpably raw anger didn't lead to a fistfight. The following day I called Ralph into my office to find out what went wrong.

"Nobody touches my pocket, Chap," he said. "It was the place my uncle put candy after he sexually abused me. I was seven years old when it started. When I was nine, my cousin and my mother started abusing me too. I tried to protect my little brother but couldn't. When I was eleven, I tried to kill myself. Some days I wish I had."

As he left, Ralph turned and said, "I'll apologize to Alan. I'll try to do better. I know Jesus would want me to."

He did do better. Ralph kept his job in the plant and stayed free of disciplinary write-ups for months. Then one day after his shift he stopped by my office to tell me about his lunchtime incident.

"I was sitting at my table talking to Santos. We were talking about Jesus's words about turning the other cheek and loving your enemy. Santos said it takes a strong man to do that. I said you sometimes got to fight back because you can't let anyone do you wrong. Then a guy on the other side of the room, a guy I had some problems with in the past, stood up and fired a spoonful of food that landed right on my tray. I was mad. I was ready to go after him. But Santos was sitting next to me. He said, 'Don't do it, man. Don't do it. Jesus wouldn't want you to do it.' And I didn't. I didn't go after him. Then Santos said, 'Come on, let's go.' And we picked up our trays and went back to work. Incredible, huh?"

"Absolutely incredible, Ralph," I said. "And how'd you feel?"

"Terrible. I still wanted to kill him."

"But you didn't kill him! That's good. That's real good."

"Yeah. Good thing Santos was there. Don't think I could've done it without him."

Inner Strength

One of the inmates was a thoughtful young man, only twenty-six years old with a life sentence. He mostly kept to himself in many ways, read a lot, and liked to write. We'd been talking about Buddhism and later he shared this reflection:

Ever thought about the Buddhist monks and the way they live their lives? They go away to a far off place, live alone, without women, without possessions, without money, without much food, without TV, without kids, and they find peace. Well, of course. Who wouldn't find it if everything is taken away that gives us human beings problems? What about us who go into battle every day? What about us who go into the mess of things every day? What about us who have mud on our clothes, blood on our face, knees knocked out from under us. . . . going into the battlefield everyday. . . . and we find the peace that passes understanding. Now, that's really something. Now that's worth talking about. Now that's a sign of God.

Some guys here are like the monks. They keep to themselves, go to eat, go to their cell, and never interact with anyone. They stay out of trouble, but they don't live their lives. I want to live my life. . . . even if it hurts . . . and find the peace there. That's the peace that passes any kind of understanding.

I don't like to read about prison life, and how to "make it" in prison. It's like asking a blind man what it's like to be blind. He doesn't need to be telling people all the time. He just wants to live his life. He is more than his circumstances.

Some people come into this prison and say they feel sorry for us because we have lost our identity here. They say that because we have no choice about our clothes, our food, our cell, our schedule. But is that what makes my identity. . . . the clothes I wear, the food I eat, the place I live, the schedule I keep? I thought it was about my spirit, my personality. I have not lost my identity. I am still who I am.

The Wisdom of Lady Galadriel

As I greeted the men at the door for the midweek Christian service, I was surprised to see Blake, a regular in the Wiccan group.

"Chap, I didn't come for the service. I came to see you. I gotta see you now."

Ushering him into my office, he started talking even before he sat down. "You got some time? Oh, hell, it doesn't matter.

This is life or death. I wanna kill a guy."

Accustomed to such impulsive threats, I simply asked, "Anyone in particular?"

The gap in his front teeth made a runway for his tongue to push his words through. "Yeah, a guy on my block. He called me a liar and a snitch. I gotta stand up to him. I gotta keep my good name."

Blake's good name was usually associated with words like annoying and mouthy. I told him it sounded like his mind was already made up.

"Well, I started thinking about it," he said. "I got six years left, and if I do this guy in, even if I just beat him up real bad, I'll get more time. And I got plans once I get outta here. So I figured that I'd come see you first and see if you have any ideas."

"Can you just avoid this guy?"

"No way. I hear his lies about me, and I just wanna smash him."

"But you haven't yet. That's good. What does your religion tell you?"

"This got nothin' to do with religion." Blake anchored his arms on top of his crossed legs. "Oh, I see what you're tryin' to do. You want me to say that Wiccans believe in 'respect all life.' You want me to say that my religion says 'don't hurt anyone.' But Chap, that's just not practical. You can't believe what we're up against in here. If I don't stand up to this guy, then everybody'll think I'm weak. No can do."

"Why do you give a flyin' fig what that guy thinks about you? Blake, didn't you tell me that you liked reading *The Lord of the Rings?* Remember when they were going into battle and they were sure that their enemy would destroy them? Lady Galadriel said, 'Hope remains while the company is true.' You got some buddies to hang in there with you. Let that guy go. I'll bet you can come up with something."

He jumped out of his chair and headed for the door. "That's it!" He stomped one foot and then the other, chanting, "Hope remains while the company is true." I wasn't sure what I'd just witnessed and can't say I held out a great deal of hope for him.

The next afternoon Blake returned with news from the front lines. "Chap, I talked to my buddies. Then I sat up all night thinking about it. I even thought about some stuff I did in the past and how I made things worse. I didn't wanna do time in lock-up over this guy. So when the canteen opened I bought two cups of coffee and a bag of chips. Then I asked the guy if he wanted coffee, and we sat down at a table. I opened up the bag of chips and said, 'Hey man, why don't we just lay this stuff down?' He just kinda smiled and kept drinking the coffee. Then he ate all the chips. And that was it."

"That *was* it!"

"Thanks, Chap. Just thought you should know." He left with a wave, and saying again, *Hope remains while the company is true!*

Imagine This

One time when the guys were lined up for smudging, a little alarm went off in my head when I spotted Genaro. "Genaro, can I talk to you for a minute?" He smiled and nodded.

The shade of the building sheltered us from the blistering noonday sun and got us out of hearing range of the other men. "Genaro, you know that you must either go into the circle to smoke the pipe, or stay outside the circle by yourself. Last week I noticed that another guy sat with you outside the circle. If custody staff sees that, they assume you're passing tobacco."

A glint of sun struck his face as he erupted. "Who told you to say this to me? You racist like everybody. You discriminating against Latinos. I write a grievance. You pickin' on me. Why you say to me? I just helpin' a brother. I not passing tobacco. I got no contraband. What you say I doin'?"

He turned away, his arms flailing with each billowing Spanish word that I didn't need a translator to understand. A dozen Latinos broke their line and encircled him. I walked closer to them, clutching my radio. Officers who could have offered assistance were inside a locked door on the other side of the building, exactly where I wanted to be at that moment. My eyes squinted as I held my gaze on the group and my finger on the radio. Genaro had tapped into his anger—for him, an endless renewable energy—and he wanted others to join him.

But instead the men grabbed his thrashing arms and pulled them down by his side. One man rested a hand on his shoulder. A chorus of voices shouted through his yelling. They stopped him. He shrugged them all away and found a place in the grass to sit alone.

Crisis averted, I sat back down in the shade to watch the men offer their prayers. I offered some of my own, praying first that my heart would dislodge from my throat. By the end, I was thinking I needed to sound a warning. I was convinced that I should chide, instruct, and impress on them the dire consequences of their outbursts—and retrieve my reputation as a fair-minded person.

I asked Juan if he would translate for clarity. He agreed, but as he stepped beside me, he whispered, "Chap, could you let it go today? Jus' let us take care of things our way. I assure you this isn't gonna happen again. Let us deal with this brother. We've got our prison ways to deal with things."

"I know some of those ways. I'll agree on the condition that no one—and I mean no one—gets hurt. Okay?"

"*Sí, sí, sí.*"

It's not my instinct, but I remained silent until we entered the building. Then I asked Genaro to come to my office. He had no choice but to follow me. He remained steely jawed as I invited him to sit down.

"No. I stand."

"Okay. That's fine. Stand if you like. I just have one question. What's your favorite song?"

He cocked his head. "What?"

I asked him again.

"John Lennon. 'Imagine.'"

"Really?" I asked. "You're so young."

"*Sí*, but my parents play Beatles a lot in my house growing up. I always like them."

I quickly found the song on my computer and played it.

Imagine there's no countries
It isn't hard to do
Nothing to kill or die for
And no religion too
Imagine all the people
Living life in peace . . .

You may say I'm a dreamer
But I'm not the only one
I hope someday you'll join us
And the world will be as one

The song ended. Genaro smiled as he extended his hand for a handshake. He said, "I love you, Chaplain."

Imagine that.

14

Struggling and Cherishing

*You have to cherish the world at the same
time you struggle to endure it.*

—Flannery O'Connor, *The Habit of Being*

In the quiet of my office at the beginning of each day, I listened to the same meditative song—*The Deer's Cry*, an ancient prayer attributed to Saint Patrick . . .

*I arise today through God's strength to pilot me.
From all who would wish me ill afar and a-near,
alone and in a multitude, against every cruel and merciless
power
that may oppose my body and my soul . . . Christ with me.*

The song pushed back the constricting walls to create an expansive space of peace within me. I prayed the same for everyone there. I was ready to face the day.

Roscoe pushed a plastic cart filled with plants from the greenhouse into my office. He reminded me of the baker I worked for as a teenager, a sizable man with ample girth and the ability to balance a six-layer cake in one hand. Roscoe was serving up potted plants, placing them on top of my bookcase, file cabinet, and desk. Each one had a name, a story, and instructions for care.

"This one'll need to be in the sun on this side," he explained as he placed the rubber plant next to the window. "It was grafted from another plant, so it's a little weak right now, but I think it'll do fine here. You've got to talk to your plants, though. They need love. They do best when they're cared for."

With each plant in their spot, Roscoe made sure to tell me their proper names. "*Spathiphyllum* is a peace lily. *Dracaena*, dragon tree. *Echeveria*, hen and chicks. *Sanseviera*, the snake plant." His teacher insisted that her students memorize those difficult Latin names.

"She told us that we could travel anywhere in the world and ask for a *crassula* and they'd bring a jade plant. I like to imagine the whole world talking through plants someday. Imagine going to an enemy country and instead of meeting them with guns, ask them, 'Do you have *Sanseviera*?'" Fiddling with the dirt of the snake plant, he said, "But that's not going to happen because we'll always find ways to kill each other. Makes me sad. We're never going to get it right, are we?"

He took off his glasses and dabbed his eyes on his shirt sleeve. "Sorry to cry, Chap. I don't mean to. I cry pretty easy. I know it bothers a lot of people. They told me that I shouldn't cry so much because I'll be considered weak, and that's not a good thing around here. But I don't care. There's a lot to cry about."

I offered Roscoe a chair and a cup of coffee, with the extra cream and sugar he liked. "Plants help me though. So does medicine. Can you tell I'm bipolar?"

A therapist suggested that he read the classics to help him through the rough patches so Roscoe told me about reading *Uncle Tom's Cabin*, how he didn't think Tom should be thought of as an "Uncle Tom," not submissive the way folks talk about that now.

"I think Tom was misunderstood," he said.

"Like you?"

"Yeah, like me. Gotta be strong to keep on a cover of your true feelings. Only way to survive."

On his way out, he patted the pot of the peace lily. "Some plants need to be pot-bound because if you put them in too big a pot their roots will start reaching out to find their edges, their boundaries, trying to get an awareness of their surroundings, their limitations. When a plant hits the side of its pot, it feels secure. It needs that. It gives it a solid foundation so it can focus on growing."

As he reached the door he turned to tell me one last thing. "All plants need similar things—air, water, dirt—but each one has special needs for light, water, and care of their leaves."

"Just like us, Roscoe. Just like all of us."

Unlike the people in prison, I was able to walk through the exit door each night into another world with light, water, and care in abundance. I could rely on the healing balm of friends, family, and a community to bolster my wilting spirit. I could take reviving walks on mountain trails, and place flowers on my dining room table. I was rich with ways to restore my soul.

But intractable systems take their toll. Though I leaned heavily on hopeful stories of personal perseverance, my well-being was like everyone else, entangled in the harshness of the environment. Acts of generosity and compassion let in the light regularly in that concrete world. Evidence was all around of people working and living within those walls who leaned toward the light of goodness. Yet over time I started losing my capacity to witness and withstand the little crucifixions of a dehumanizing system. A soul weariness set in. Plus my aging body was feeling the strains of a long commute. It was time to leave.

The Human Spirit

As I packed up my office, I sorted through files of letters, little missives that had arrived in my mailbox from men who no longer had anyone to read them. At the halfway mark of his forty-year sentence, one man wrote, "The human spirit is a remarkable thing. With it we are empowered to endure, when enduring seems utterly impossible. With it we are made strong, even when everything around us is constructed to make us weak. When all of life has pressed us down, it is the human spirit—in its relentless effort to survive, to endure, to grow— that elevates us once again to a level where our human dignity becomes apparent."

I held small items tucked in my desk drawers, pausing over each gift and remembering the faces of the men who gave them to me. There was a pair of tiny, shining silver shoes crafted from a potato chip bag, with the word *peace* penned on the heels, referring to the passage in Isaiah, "How beautiful upon the mountains are the feet of those who proclaim peace, who bring good tidings." There were crosses woven out of twisted plastic garbage bags or bent coffee stirrers. There were cards with drawings of flowers or paper-shaped butterflies. With unending hours stretching in front of them, many inmates made works of art from throw-away things—signs of the universal longing to create and to give, no matter how limited the resources.

As I packed my books, my companions for the journey— Etty Hillesum, Howard Thurman, and others—I noticed a note stuck in one of them. It was from Chap Bill, written in the aftermath of my "Below Good" rating. He wrote, "Sometimes I regret that I ever introduced you to the prison system. Some of my sadness and regret about my prison chaplaincy days is that I grew numb to the 'junk' that happened." He wished he had done more to expose the wrongs and injustices but "maybe it's not too late," he added. He closed his note with encouragement: "I have faith and hope that the Spirit will lead you through all this . . . just remember that there is more in this life, beyond our imagination, much more than this."

I experienced the "more in this life" beyond my imaginings in my chaplaincy. A snow angel, a reggae concert, a blessing word—I wondered what we would remember of one another. Some of their faces I see even now, their stories linked together in a kind of rosary of memory, each leading to the next. I wonder about their many days of feeling "below good." I wonder if, by some miracle of grace, some have come to know themselves as "beyond good"—knowing the love of God in that mysterious way that brings a peace that passes all understanding.

We can never fully know the impact our intersected lives make on each other. Seeing the significance of an encounter barely remembered can startle us into gratitude. One inmate sent me a note in his barely legible handwriting that a simple prayer we had shared together was his "jump start": "Ever since that day I am not where I want to be, but neither am I where I used to be. God put that on your heart to say that prayer for me." I echoed his words—not where I want to be, but a long way from where I used to be.

I took another picture off the wall, a framed piece that my husband had given to me with a quote from Reed Levertov: "The last person to whom Jesus spoke was a convicted felon, and he did so to offer forgiveness and absolution."

Kicking Doe

On my last day, the staff acknowledged my service with a reception, where they presented me with three plaques: one from the governor of North Carolina bearing the state seal; one called the Old North State Award, for employees who stay a decade or more; and one from my colleagues bearing the words "The Chaplaincy Office has been forever changed. In recognition of the person you are, a love gift has been given to Freedom Life Ministries"—a transitional ministry for returning citizens from prison.

No turkey sandwiches were served, which I thought was a missed opportunity. My boss, however, did tell me that he would miss me. How dull his days must have been after my leaving.

I went back to my office and carefully placed the *Spathi-phyllum*, the peace plant, in a box. I tucked the plaques in another box, next to a certificate signed by the Native American inmates. I sat for a moment to savor the memory of the day I received it.

It had been a warm spring day after a particularly harsh winter. How wonderful it was to finally go outside to the sacred circle without a heavy coat. As I watched the pipe ceremony begin to unfold, I noticed a regular participant sitting on the grass. I asked him why he was not joining the group. "My spirit is full of too many hurts and too much anger this week. I don't want to infect the others," he explained. "But I need to hear the prayers."

I shuddered to think how many times I had contaminated groups with my agitated spirit. But that day the blue-canopied sky gave me a sense of peace.

At the end of the prayers, Tokala, the pipe-bearer, offered an unusual invitation. "Come join us in the circle," he said gently to me. Surprised, I walked clockwise around the circle to the entrance. Waving a feather over a smoking seashell, Tokala smudged me with sage and motioned for me to stand close to the center.

He swirled a dab of cornmeal and water in the palm of his hand. Then he marked my forehead with the paste. "Chap, we've decided to give you a new name today. We name you 'Kicking Doe,' to honor your fighting spirit and gentle heart."

The men stood for a prayer to the Creator. Then forearm handshakes of congratulations commenced as they chanted, "Kicking Doe. Kicking Doe." They were smiling. I think I was smiling. I know I was kicking back tears.

I drove from the prison parking lot at dusk that day, just as the sky was changing color to soft orange and pink. As I rounded a curve toward a bank of deep evergreens, I spotted a doe standing by the roadside. I'd never seen a deer before in those trees. The doe stood alone. Her eyes caught mine. Then she kicked up her heels and dashed into the forest.

The next day I saw two of the Native American inmates in the hallway. I told them about my surprise visitation. "I saw a doe!" I cried. "Can you believe that?"

They smiled, nodded, and walked away without a word.

Epilogue

Marked for Life

I dwell in possibility. . .

—Emily Dickinson

"Chap, you got a minute?" Dozens of inmates passed through the corridor around us, but Slate just looked at his watch. Sixty seconds passed. "That's it," he said. "You gave me a minute. I'm eternally grateful for your time." He smiled as he joined the flow of inmates on their way to work. I watched them walk away and thought about Slate, this man who'd barely known a second of peace in his life, starting with being choke-chained in an attic for being a recalcitrant six-year-old. Slate, the inmate who told me after choir one day that it looked like I could use a "snow angel"—so he threw his large body onto the carpeted floor and started sweeping his arms and legs back and forth. He got up and said, "There! Isn't that the prettiest snow angel you've ever seen?"

"Yes, I do believe it's the best one I've ever seen, especially in the heat of summer."

I imagined asking for a minute to greet all the newcomers to our prison. I wanted to stand at the receiving dock with the words: *Welcome. The cruelty and abuse that has been done to you or that you have done to yourself or others stops here. Here we practice a new way of being human together. Here we stop blaming. Here we practice taking responsibility for your life, and we practice respect for yourself and others. Your story is not over. Change is possible. God is here. Peace to you. Come on in.*

There were staff and administrators who made efforts to carry forth such a vision. Yet even when respect and encouragement were given, the system could be a monumental hindrance toward the restoration of lives. The gravitational pull from social and personal patterns of behavior was fierce. But one thing became clear: the human spirit cannot withstand perpetual powerlessness. There will be an uprising.

I never experienced anything but safety in my own home. I grew up afraid of wasps and scorpions. I was never afraid that my parents would slam me against a wall, beat me with a bat, or chain me to a fence. I didn't fear the darkness of a bedroom with marauding molesters. I never imagined that I might die by a gun or a knife. I didn't worry about being belittled or abused by parents who were drugged or drunk. I didn't know anyone who dropped out of school or ended up in prison. My neighborhoods weren't raided by law enforcement. I wasn't targeted for suspicion or arrest because of my skin color. I didn't experience the daily traumas of addiction or mental illness.

When the main thoroughfares of society were blocked to the inmates, they found detours and pathways of survival, sometimes making the only choice that seemed available to them. But I also held hope that their self-defeating and abusive choices could be exchanged for good and redeeming ones.

I can testify to acts of mercy and goodness when I least expected it. I received a twenty-six–page letter of hatred from an inmate who was certain that I was the worst chaplain in the state. A simple note of "I don't like you" would have sufficed. He bragged about his letter to a couple of inmates out on the yard. A few days later I received a gift of twenty-seven pages of gratitude from twenty-seven inmates. Goodness prevailed. I was grateful.

So many times during those years I thought of the words in Proverbs 18: *The human spirit will endure sickness, but a broken spirit, who can bear?* For the inmates, the staff, for me—even the best of intentions could be swept out to sea in the undertows of despairing times.

I lost hope for a while. I retraced my steps to find it. Did I lose it in the hospital room when I visited an officer whose jaw had been dislocated by an inmate? Or was it the day I fled from my segregation visit because the smell of feces smeared on a cell wall made me nauseous? Was it the conversation with the inmate who was in four-point restraints because the staff had grown tired of his verbal tirades? Was it that incident when the medical team valiantly treated the inmate whose neck had been slashed open by an inmate I'd considered non-violent? Or maybe it was the time I led a workshop for a regional staff meeting on the topic, "How to Treat an Inmate Like a Human Being" and no one came.

I stepped onto my small stage like an improvisational actor. I took what was presented to me and sought to create a presence that was life affirming. But the particularities could get lost in the similarities. My heartbeat of concern flatlined when I listened to the agonies of someone's story and assumed I'd heard it before. It simply was not true. Everyone had a unique story to tell and to live.

Some staff said, "I don't want to know their crime. It might change the way I treat them." I wanted to know their crime because it might change the way I understood them. Their crime was part of them and an honest avenue toward healing. As a chaplain I had a unique relationship that allowed me to enter into their lives. I wanted to hear the stories they rarely told, the ones that were not rote and reeled off to every case manager, court-appointed attorney, or administrator. I wanted to know when they knew they mattered to someone, and someone mattered to them. I asked for stories of their heroes, their hopes, their joys. Together we sifted through the ruins to find what remained for a new start.

"We've got the mark of Cain, and we'll never be rid of it," was the lament of some inmates, sure that it symbolized shame, failure, and banishment. But instead of a curse for killing his brother Abel, the mark of Cain was given as a sign of protection from God against the vengeance of others. It was a mark for life, not death. It was the mercy mark.

Mercy. It was my one-word prayer, the plea I found myself saying daily, repeatedly, in a kind of pray-without-ceasing kind of way. Sometimes I said the word audibly. Mostly it was my inner cry.

Mercy is not going soft on crime. It doesn't flinch from our cruelties and deceptions. It doesn't avoid looking at the constellation of people still suffering the aftermath of crimes, from grieving parents, to bewildered children, to surviving victims, to a wounded community. The miracle of mercy is that it can be clear-eyed to our hatreds and horrors but still interrupt our ceaseless rounds of retaliation and vengeance.

Mercy is not mercy if it is given to those who deserve it. Mercy is an opening into the possibility for transformation. It can carry the full weight of our failings. It is a holy gift that can enable us to begin again. It seeks the healing of the wounds for victims, perpetrators, and community alike.

We play no small part in this work. The longing for vengeance, which we all feel when violated, whether large or small, is rooted in the demand for justice. But retaliation almost always escalates the cycle of violence, until it becomes self-perpetuating; an eye not just for an eye, but for a piece of scalp, too, and on and on until the whole world is not simply blind but irrevocably battered and broken.

Luke found his part in the work of mercy and became a "bless-er." I often reminded the inmates that they had the power to curse or to bless. Luke decided God wanted him to bless. He made it his vocation. He carried one-line blessings in his pocket, suitable for various occasions. He had blessings for inmates or staff who were grieving a death in their family. He had blessings for peace of mind amid the daily conflicts. He wrote blessings for food, visits, policies, transfers, classes, work, and weather. "Chap, you need a blessing? I got one for you." Skimming the words from his pocketed papers, he found one for the moment. "May your acts of kindness and mercy be rewarded by seeing God smile in the face of someone whose need was met."

It is not difficult to experience awe in the beauty of a sunset, but it is a true wonder of the world to see a fist become a handshake. It is a miracle to see a bag of potato chips become a means of peacemaking. It is breathtaking to see curses turn to blessings. It is stunning to see disasters diverted by calm and wisdom. We could see more of such wonders if restoration of broken lives was our common cause.

We carry within us the power to bless and to redeem. Society can change if we revise our narrative about crime and punishment to emphasize the transformation of lives. We were the people who designed and created these places of punishment. We can reimagine them into becoming places of promise and possibility.

I bore witness to lives shaped by curses and blessings. I sought to make sense of things, even when nothing did.

Standing beside people in their furies and their failures, I was pushed to see my own. When I witnessed hope rising from the ruins, I rose again too. A truth emerged that embraces us all. Each of us is a part of a greater story that is wider and deeper than our own. We need each other to become more human and more humane. Unchangeable things can change, around us, even within us, even now. The world still shimmers with the presence of God.